paradise
Stitched
Sashiko & Appliqué Quilts

Sylvia Pippen

C&T PUBLISHING

Text copyright © 2009 by Sylvia Pippen

Artwork copyright © 2009 by C&T Publishing, Inc.

Publisher: Amy Marson

Creative Director: Gailen Runge

Editors: Liz Aneloski and Cynthia Bix

Technical Editors: Ann Haley and
Sandy Peterson

Copyeditor/Proofreader: Wordfirm Inc.

Cover/Book Designer: Kristy Zacharias

Production Coordinator: Kirstie L.
Pettersen

Illustrator: Aliza Shalit

Photography by Christina Carty-Francis
and Diane Pedersen of C&T Publishing,
Inc., unless otherwise noted.

Published by C&T Publishing, Inc., P.O. Box 1456, Lafayette, CA 94549

Library of Congress Cataloging-in-Publication Data

Pippen, Sylvia

Paradise stitched—Sashiko and appliqué quilts / Sylvia Pippen.

p. cm.

Includes bibliographical references.

Summary: "A guide to making quilts using a combination of Sashiko and appliqué techniques. Step-by-step instructions and full-size patterns for 6 quilts with colorful tropical
themes. Includes a gallery"--Provided by publisher.

ISBN 978-1-57120-617-6 (paper trade : alk. paper)

1. Appliqué--Patterns. 2. Sashiko. 3. Quilting. I. Title.

TT779.P358 2009

746.44'5041--dc22

2008050943

Printed in China

10 9 8 7 6 5

contents

dedications

Aloha to my loving partner, Peter; to our children Amy, Brian, and Kim; and to our grandchildren, Samantha, Matthew, and Troy. To my father and mother, Eldon and Kitty Pippen, who taught me the joy of working with my hands.

To all of my students, who continue to inspire me to be a better teacher.

To Julie Yukimura of Kapaia Stitchery on Kauai, whose generous legacy to the quilt community lives on.

acknowledgments

This book has been a family affair and could not have been written without my family's continuous encouragement and help along the way. A big *mahalo* to my partner, Peter Millington, who gave up his shop to make me a beautiful quilting studio; to our son, Brian Koenig, and my cousin Susie Stanley for their artistic expertise; to my brother, David Pippen, for his computer advice; to my sister, Nancy, for her exquisite Fimo miniatures of quilters; and to our daughter Amy Koenig for her business consulting. Finally, *mahalo nui loa* to my mother for her countless hours of sage advice, her help with assembling quilts, and a lifetime of one-on-one Kitty Pippen workshops.

foreword
by Kitty Pippen

Sharing my passion for quilting with Sylvia gives me great joy!

Something wonderful happened when we started working together. Although our specialized interests differed, we were soon exchanging helpful ideas. For many years, I had been studying Japanese fabrics and using them almost exclusively in my quilts. Sylvia, on the other hand, wanted to make textile versions of flowers, birds, and sea life inspired from her life in Hawaii. As time went on, we made many quilts together, co-authored a book, traveled to teach at retreats, and showed our quilts. And now Sylvia has designed many patterns and written this book with useful ideas for making innovative quilts.

A mother's heartfelt gratitude, pride, and love go to my daughter, Sylvia.

Kitty Pippen

Eloise Taniguchi,
Waimea, Kauai

Catherine Wilson,
Waimea, Kauai

Ely and Hoku Barat,
Waimea, Kauai

introduction

I live in Hawaii, surrounded by exuberant tropical flowers and an azure blue ocean. Inspiration abounds right out the door of my studio, where our garden overflows with bananas, plumeria, giant heliconia, and a host of native and exotic plants. I've been a gardener most of my life, and quilting is an extension of my passion for plants. I am compelled to make quilts that reflect the beauty and diversity of the Islands.

In keeping with the polyglot culture of Hawaii, I like to mix up quilt traditions—a Tahitian curved border, a Japanese wave design, and the symmetry of Hawaiian quilts. I was introduced to Japanese design, Sashiko, and the fine art of quiltmaking by my mother, Kitty Pippen, who has been my inspiration and mentor all my life.

I love to teach and introduce Sashiko to students of all ages. When I lived on the west side of Kauai, I taught weekly classes at Nana's House, where students from the age of 8 to 80 gathered to create their own Sashiko designs. Breaking from Japanese Sashiko tradition, they wanted to work in lots of color and use designs that reflected life in Hawaii, such as hukilaus of tropical fish caught up in a Sashiko net, or fragrant butter-yellow plumeria. From my wonderful students, I learned how to work with diverse ages, abilities, and the true meaning of aloha. I encourage you to use Sashiko not only as a teaching tool but also for your own artistic expression. As you will see, Sashiko can be adapted to any design. And remember, it isn't how perfect your stitches are but how much you enjoy the journey along the way.

sashiko

traditional and contemporary sashiko

Sashiko, which means "little stabs" in Japanese, is a simple running stitch traditionally used to work intricate designs with white thread on indigo fabric. Sashiko has been a compelling and practical art form for centuries and was originally used to strengthen and sandwich layers of cloth for warmth in northern Japan.

Traditional Sashiko designs abound. Kamon, or family crests, and natural objects, such as cherry blossoms or cranes, are stylized into dozens of variations. Geometric designs, all with ancient historical meanings, are also well suited to Sashiko.

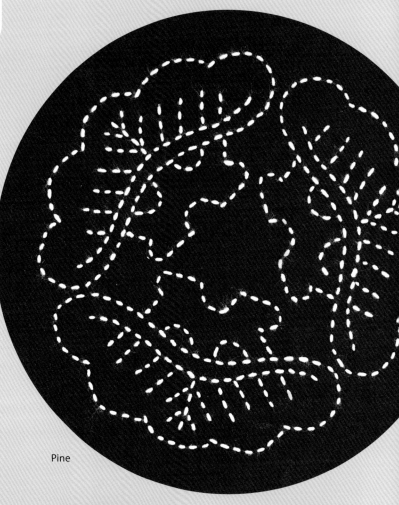

Pine

Lotus

Double crane

Wisteria

Feathers

Kamon crests

My mother grew up in China, where this lattice design (left) was commonly used for windows and as decorative elements in the empress of China's summer palace near Beijing.

Traditional geometric Sashiko designs of basket weaves, fretwork, intersecting circles, or curved waves are wonderful background fillers behind flowing natural shapes rendered in appliqué. Sashiko designs can also be used to sandwich quilts using quilting thread instead of Sashiko thread.

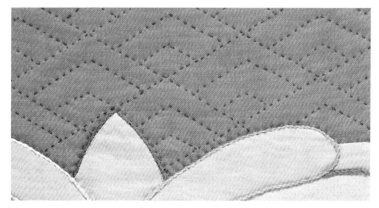

Sashiko waves used as quilting pattern; detail of *Orchid Tivaevae*, by Sylvia Pippen (page 43).

Today Sashiko has evolved from a practical art form into decorative surface embellishment, with the thread pulled through only the top layer, rather than through all three layers, of a quilt sandwich. Sashiko can stand alone or dramatically complement pieced or appliqué quilts. The beauty of Sashiko is its simplicity: A humble running stitch can outline the most intricate design. I use traditional Japanese geometrics and Kamon crests in my quilts but am continually discovering new twists to this old art form.

Maple leaf border; detail of *Wildflowers and Sashiko*, by Sylvia Pippen (page 46).

Chinese Sashiko Lattice, by Kitty Pippen

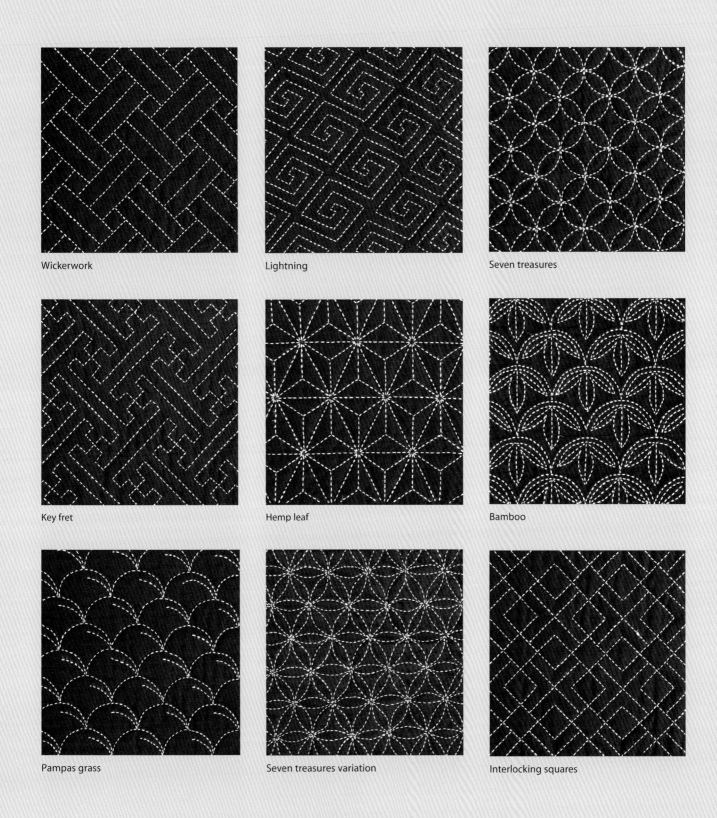

Wickerwork

Lightning

Seven treasures

Key fret

Hemp leaf

Bamboo

Pampas grass

Seven treasures variation

Interlocking squares

Geometric Sashiko designs

Hand-appliqued waves (top), and waves outlined in Sashiko (bottom); details of *Tropical Sea Life Sampler* by Sylvia Pippen (page 45)

Seashells and Sashiko, 18˝ × 18˝, by Sylvia Pippen (see Resources, page 78, for quilt pattern information)

Although Sashiko lines can be stitched by machine, the machine's continuous stitching line does not give the soft look of hand Sashiko, in which stitches have space between them that allows the background to show. If you are a machine quilter, I encourage you to try hand Sashiko. You might be surprised at how fast it goes and how calming it is to sit down and stitch a beautiful Sashiko design.

Kamon crests, such as the waves, can be modified by adding hand or machine appliqué within the design. Complicated shapes can be filled in using fusible appliqué and finished with decorative, satin-stitched machine appliqué that is then outlined in hand Sashiko.

Machine-appliquéd waves; detail of *Tropical Sea Life Sampler*, by Sylvia Pippen (page 45)

sashiko supplies

Sashiko requires very few supplies beyond a sharp needle with a big eye, thread, scissors, suitable fabric, and perhaps a sturdy thimble. No hoop is required. Your Sashiko project is easy to carry along and can be done anywhere, even in less-than-optimal light.

SASHIKO THREAD

Japanese Sashiko thread is made of loosely twisted, long-staple cotton. This type of cotton is very strong and comes in many colors and in fine, medium, and thick weights. Perle cotton #8 and #5, embroidery floss, crochet thread, and silk are alternative threads. Experiment to find what works best for your project.

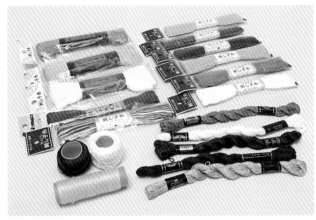

Sashiko threads

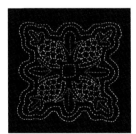

Colored Sashiko thread used in *Pineapple (left)* and *Cherry Blossoms (right)*, both by Nancy Taniguchi

NEEDLES

The right Sashiko needle will make your stitching enjoyable and will eliminate wear and tear on your hands. Unlike quilting thread, Sashiko thread is thick and bulky, so the needle has to pierce a hole in the fabric large enough to easily pull through two thicknesses of thread and the eye of the needle. Sashiko needles are very sharp, thick, and strong and come in different lengths and thicknesses. Experiment with different size needles and types of fabric. If one needle is too hard to pull, try another size. Alternatively, you can use embroidery or crewel needles.

It is also important to choose a needle with the right thickness and length for your project. For tightly woven fabrics, use shorter and smaller needles. For looser-weave fabrics, use longer needles so you can gather more stitches at a time. Thimbles are optional.

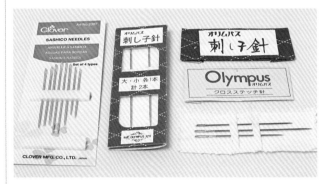

Sashiko needles

FABRICS FOR SASHIKO

Sashiko was traditionally stitched on hand-dyed indigo cotton, linen, hemp, or other plant fibers. Don't use true indigo dyed fabric if you are going to combine it with appliqué, as the indigo may bleed when washed. Some reproduction indigos and sturdy commercial cottons are dye-fast. Avoid using batiks, as the thread count is too fine for Sashiko.

Fabrics for Sashiko and appliqué backgrounds

creating the sashiko

MARKING THE DESIGN

The easiest way to mark Sashiko designs on dark fabric is to use a waxless, white transfer paper. Be sure to test your transfer paper first to make sure it produces a clean line and does not smear. Mark carefully—not all transfer paper markings will wash out.

1. Place the transfer paper with the white side down on top of the fabric. Position the pattern on top of the transfer paper.

2. Pin on one side of the pattern, through all 3 layers, and mark part of a pattern line using a stylus, a fine lead pencil, or a ballpoint pen. Open on the pin hinge to make sure the line is transferring well. The hinge allows you to check your line without disturbing the pattern's placement.

3. Pin all 4 corners outside the design. Trace and transfer the design.

If a Sashiko design has a simple shape or curve, trace the shape onto template plastic or cardstock. Then cut out the shape and use a chalk pencil to trace around the pattern onto dark fabric.

Geometric designs with straight lines can be transferred using a ruler and transfer paper or by marking a grid on the fabric with a chalk pencil.

PREPARING SASHIKO THREAD

1. Open the skein and remove the paper band.

2. Look for the extra loop around the skein; cut through all threads at this point.

3. Cut the other end of the loop.

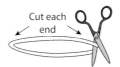

Cut each end

4. You will have 2 separate bundles of thread. Flip one of the bundles 180°. Sashiko threads have a twist; flipping one bundle will ensure that the twist is going the same way throughout the bundle.

5. Hold onto the entire bundle and pull out a thread. Cut the thread into 3 pieces and use these pieces of thread to tightly tie the bundle in 3 places with square knots.

Tie in 3 places

Sashiko thread tends to fray, so use lengths of thread no longer than 20″–24″.

STITCHING A SASHIKO DESIGN

1. Either pull a thread from your traditional Sashiko thread bundle or cut a 20″–24″ length of perle cotton or other thread. Thread this through the large eye of a sharp needle and make a single knot at the end.

2. Bring the threaded needle up from the back of the marked background fabric. You may start stitching at any point along the design, but do plan a stitching route that does not require too many twists, turns, or long skipped spaces on the back.

3. Place the point of the needle flat on the design line a short distance from the point at which the thread emerges; measure this distance. This will help you gauge how long the stitches should be before you pull the needle through the fabric. If the needle is angled or held straight up before taking a stitch, the point may not stay on line or you may misjudge the stitch length.

> ### stitching tip
> In Japanese sewing, the needle is held still and the fabric placed on it in a pleating action. Put some light tension on the fabric and rock it, gathering several stitches onto the needle.

4. Take 2–3 stitches onto the needle. Keep the length of the stitch the same (5–7 stitches per inch). Traditionally, the stitch on top is slightly longer than the space in between. However, evenness is more important than stitch length.

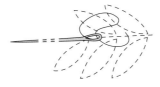

Stitch length

5. Pull the needle and thread through to the knot.

6. After stitching an inch or two, pull up on the thread a little. Using your thumb, carefully stretch out the stitching. The idea is to keep the work loose, especially the thread on the back, so the fabric does not pucker.

> ### ironing tip
> Always iron your finished work from the back so the Sashiko stitching isn't crushed or made shiny.

sashiko tips

Traditional Sashiko instructions provide detailed directions regarding the stitching routes to take and the number of stitches per leg of the design. As you acquire experience and confidence, you will develop your own methods. The main concern is to keep the stitches even and the lines smooth. Here are a few tips:

• A stitch must end at the turn of a corner, with the thread either going to the back or coming up to the top. To stitch tight curves, shorten the stitches slightly.

Corner and circle

• Threads that skip across the back should not measure longer than ½″. Leave the strand loose on the back to avoid puckering. Sometimes a longer skip can be avoided by weaving the thread through several stitches on the back to reach a new section of the marked design.

Skip across the back of the work

• To finish off a line of stitching, pull the threaded needle through the back and weave the thread tail through several stitches before clipping the thread.

Finish off threads

appliqué methods

I encourage you to experiment with different appliqué techniques, because each method has something specific to offer. For example, paper piecing works well for precise geometric shapes, while needle-turn appliqué is great for big free-form shapes. My current favorite is the press-over heat-resistant Mylar method, because it offers an easy way to form crisp intricate shapes that are ready to appliqué. Quilters who find hand appliqué intimidating can easily master the Mylar method. All the appliqué patterns in this book can also be adapted to machine appliqué using fusible adhesive.

press-over mylar method

For this easy method, you start by tracing the appliqué shape from the pattern onto Mylar. Then you cut it out and use it to fussy cut your fabric, adding a 3/16″ turn-over seam allowance. Next, you spray the fabric shape with starch to give it extra stability and stiffness when it is time to press the seam allowance over the Mylar template. The Mylar template can be used over and over. (Step-by-step instructions follow.)

I like the Mylar method when experimenting with new designs. I can quickly form a fabric petal, pop out the Mylar template, and pin the shape to the design wall to audition it. Each appliqué shape can then be formed, tweaked, and repositioned until it is just right.

This method also makes it possible to appliqué some flowers in hand using preformed shapes, instead of working petal by petal on the background fabric. A completed flower, fish, or bird can also be embellished with embroidery before appliquéing it to the background fabric. It is much easier to turn a little flower in your hand than on a whole quilt top!

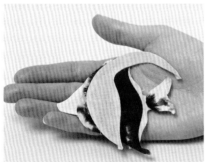

Mylar formed shapes

It is very satisfying to sit down with a stack of crisp little petals ready to appliqué. The petals fit *exactly* into the traced shape on the background, just like fitting a piece into a jigsaw puzzle. No guesswork or fighting to needle-turn a small intricate shape.

SUPPLIES

- Small craft iron: I prefer the one made by Hobbico (see Resources, page 78).

- 8½″ × 11″ sheets of thin (0.005″) matte-finish Mylar (see Resources, page 78)

- Black permanent fine-line marking pen for marking Mylar (Avoid water-based ink or pencil graphite, which can both bleed onto fabric when starch and heat are applied.)

- Chalk pencil for marking fabric

- Firm, small ironing pad

- Light-duty spray starch

- Paper towels

supply tip
Use a 6″ × 6″ square of plywood covered with ironing board fabric. A hard surface is necessary to achieve crisp edges.

TRACING APPLIQUÉ SHAPES ONTO MYLAR

1. With a fine-line permanent pen, trace the appliqué shapes onto Mylar. Do not add seam allowances when tracing the appliqué shapes onto the Mylar. Mark overlapping areas with dashed lines.

2. Mark the right side with the corresponding letter or number. It is easy to reverse the pieces, so mark "up" on the right side.

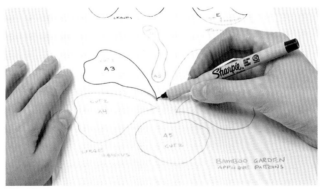

Trace appliqué shapes.

3. Cut out the Mylar template with a pair of sharp, pointed paper scissors. Be accurate; use fine sandpaper or an emery board to smooth out any lumps or bumps. Store your Mylar shapes in a small box or resealable plastic bag.

Cut out Mylar templates.

CUTTING AND PREPARING FABRIC

Refer to Fabrics for Appliqué, page 20, before cutting.

1. Place the Mylar template right side up on the right side of the fabric. With a chalk pencil, draw around the template, adding a scant ³⁄₁₆˝ press-over allowance. Don't use any marking tool that will stain your fabric when starch is applied.

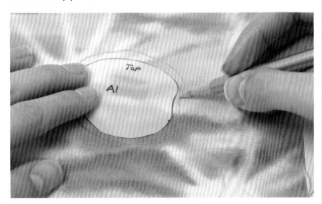

Add ³⁄₁₆˝ press-over allowance.

2. Cut out the fabric on the drawn line.

Applying Starch to Fabric

1. With the wrong side up, place the fabric shapes on a paper towel. Spray each piece with starch or use a brush to soak the entire piece with starch.

Starch wrong side of fabric shapes.

2. Blot excess moisture with another paper towel.

3. Let the pieces air dry until only slightly damp. If you apply heat too soon, the starch will get sticky and gum up your iron.

PRESSING-OVER MYLAR

1. Place the Mylar templates, wrong side up, onto the wrong side of the fabric shapes.

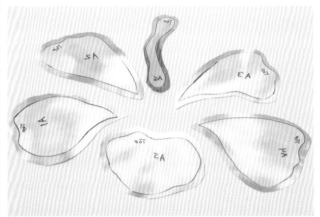

Place Mylar templates.

> *pressing tip*
> To protect your fingers, use a wooden stylus or chopstick to hold the Mylar in place.

2. Use the point of the iron to start folding and pressing the seam allowance over the Mylar. Use the edge of the iron to turn over long seam allowances. Always push the iron toward the fold-over. If you pull the iron back over your freshly pressed seam allowance, the fabric can catch and unfold. (To press points and tight curves, see facing page.)

3. Keep pushing the iron over the first sections to make sure the seam allowance is firmly pressed down.

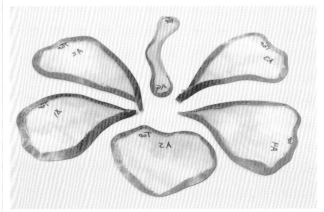

Completed press-over Mylar shapes; wrong side up

4. Remove Mylar templates.

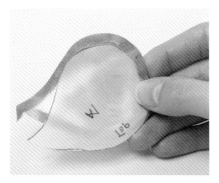

Remove Mylar template.

Completed appliqué shape, right side up, with Mylar removed

5. Refer to Traditional Appliqué Stitch (page 19) to appliqué each shape in place where indicated in the project instructions.

Points

To establish perfect points, use the tip of your iron to press over one overlap allowance at the point. Work your way around the shape until you have folded the opposite seam allowance over the point. Leave the flap; it can be trimmed just before you appliqué and will prevent fraying.

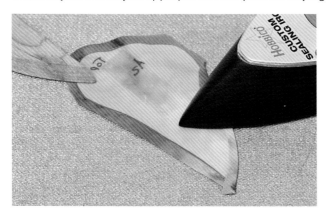

Iron over one side of point.

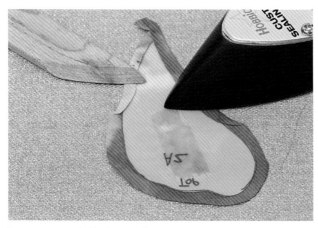

Iron over second side, leaving flap.

Tight Curves

1. Convex curves can be "gathered" over the Mylar a little at a time, using the side of the iron. If you get a hard fold, trim the seam allowance down, dab a bit of starch on that spot with your finger or a paintbrush, and iron it again.

Press convex curves.

2. Concave curves need to be clipped, unless they are on a bias that will easily stretch. To clip curves, first iron over the straight or gentle curves to fix the Mylar in place. The last step is to clip the curves, cutting within a few threads of the turn-over edge; the Mylar will serve as a stop for your scissors. With the point of your iron, fold and press down the center of the concave curve first; then work out to the outer edges.

Clip concave curves.

paper-template method

You can achieve perfectly formed shapes by hand basting the seam allowance around the edges of a paper shape. This method works well for geometric shapes, such as squares or hexagons, and for gently curved organic shapes.

1. Trace the appliqué patterns onto freezer or computer paper the number of times indicated in the project instructions for each shape. Cut out the shapes. Do not add seam allowances when tracing the appliqué shapes onto the paper.

2. Write the corresponding pattern number on the wrong side of each paper shape so you can keep track of how each piece fits into the design.

3. Pin the right side of each paper shape to the wrong side of the appropriate fabric. If the shape has a curved edge, position it on the bias grain of the fabric, as it is much easier to turn a bias edge around a curve.

4. Cut around each shape, adding a generous ¼˝ turn-under allowance all around.

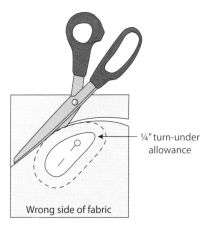

¼˝ turn-under allowance

Wrong side of fabric

Cut out each shape.

5. Fold the ¼˝ turn-under allowance onto the paper (back) side of each shape. Clip the turn-under allowance only where necessary, such as on the inside of a tight curve. Baste around the edge of each shape through all layers.

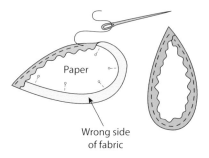

Paper

Wrong side of fabric

Fold seam allowance and baste.

6. Refer to Traditional Appliqué Stitch (facing page) to appliqué each shape in place where indicated in the project instructions, leaving open a 1˝ section. Remove the basting stitches. Remove the paper shape and finish appliquéing.

needle-turn method

Needle-turn appliqué proceeds directly from cutting the piece to appliquéing it onto the background fabric. This method works well for large appliqué shapes, such as curved borders, or for Hawaiian quilts.

1. Trace each appliqué pattern onto template plastic and cut out. Follow Steps 1–3 for Tracing Appliqué Shapes onto Mylar (page 15).

2. Place the templates right side up on the right side of the appropriate fabrics. Trace around each template with a fine-line chalk pencil. Trace as many of each shape as indicated in the project instructions.

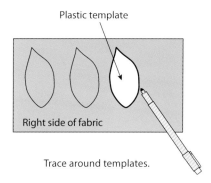

Plastic template

Right side of fabric

Trace around templates.

3. Cut out each appliqué shape, adding a ⅛″ turn-under allowance.

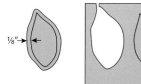

Cut out shapes.

4. Referring to the project instructions, position the first appliqué on the quilt top. Pin, baste, or glue baste the shape in place, placing the basting line well within the marked line, so the turn-under allowance can be turned under completely.

5. Using the tip of the needle, gently turn under a short length of the turn-under allowance, making sure the marked line is not visible.

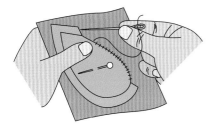

Turn under a short section.

Refer to Traditional Appliqué Stitch to stitch the turned-under portion. Continue turning under and appliquéing short sections until the entire shape is appliquéd.

6. Repeat Steps 4 and 5 to position, baste, and appliqué the remaining shapes in place in the order indicated.

fusible appliqué

Fusible appliqué is especially useful for small pieces and complicated shapes. Trace the reverse of the pattern, including any overlap extensions, onto the paper side of paper-backed fusible adhesive. Cut out the shape; do not include a seam allowance. Fuse as directed by the manufacturer. For stability, stitch around the shape along the raw edge.

traditional appliqué stitch

The trick to impeccable appliqué is to make your stitches invisible. (For a finished example, see the columbine flower on page 31.) Use a sharp, fine appliqué needle and 60-weight machine embroidery thread or extra-fine thread such as #100 silk thread that exactly matches the appliqué fabric color.

1. Beginning on a straight edge and underneath the background fabric, insert the needle into the background fabric, beneath the appliqué piece. Come up through the background fabric, just catching the edge of the appliqué.

2. Insert the needle into the background fabric, directly opposite where the thread came up and slightly over the edge of the appliqué piece. Stitches should not be more than ⅛″ long. Give the thread a slight tug every 5 or 6 stitches.

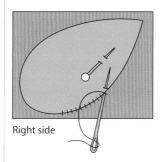
Right side

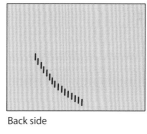
Back side

Stitch.

3. To tie off the appliqué thread, take 3 stitches side by side inside the appliqué stitch line on the back of the quilt. Use a figure-eight knot to lock the stitches in place. This is especially important when using silk thread, which can slip if not secured tightly.

Figure-eight knot

fabrics
for appliqué

choosing the fabrics

Choosing the right appliqué fabrics to set off your Sashiko design will make your quilt sparkle. The trick is to find fabrics that capture the essence of the flower, fish, or bird you are creating. Buy fat quarters or one-third yard of many fabrics to build your stash. You will be "painting" with tiny bits of fabric, so you need a broad palette.

When shopping for appliqué fabrics, take along a piece of your background fabric, so you can audition potential fabrics against it. Does the fabric look vibrant and "pop" off the background, or does it recede and look dull? What catches my eye are fabrics that look as if they have been painted with watercolors, with subtle transitions from one color to another, translucent spots, and gentle contours that suggest, for example, the ridge of a petal or the vein of a leaf.

I am always on the lookout for fabrics with flashes of true white to create the illusion of light. They are surprisingly hard to find but very effective in making flowers look luminescent.

Passionflower; detail of *Passionflower*, by Sylvia Pippen (page 39), and fabric

Columbine; detail of *North American Wildflowers & Sashiko*, by Sylvia Pippen (page 46), and fabric

Lupine and poppies; detail of *Wildflowers & Sashiko*, by Sylvia Pippen (page 46), and fabric

Ginger block; detail of *Tropical Sashiko Sampler*, by Sylvia Pippen (page 37), and fabric

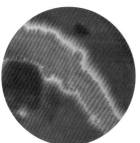

Any cotton fabric is fair game, from big ugly prints you would normally walk right by to the finest batiks.

I look at fabrics with a microscopic eye, trying to isolate tiny sections that suggest the curve of a bird's bill, the shadow under a passionflower petal, the green and red of a mango. I use lots of batiks, because they come in a huge color range, have a high thread count, and don't fray. However, I will work with any fabric, regardless of quality, if it has the color or pattern I need.

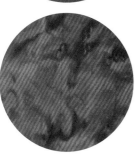

Angel trumpet; detail of *Tropical Sashiko Sampler*, by Sylvia Pippen (page 37), and fabric

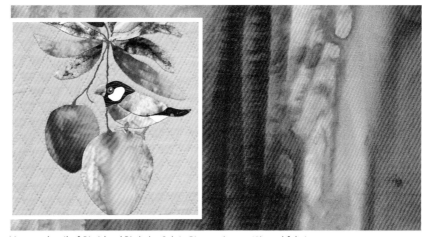

Mango; detail of *Big Island Birds*, by Sylvia Pippen (page 42), and fabric

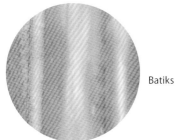

Batiks

Many hand-dyed fabrics are available. Look for ones that have distinct values of one color or multicolored gradations in small scale. Marbled fabrics are unsurpassed for butterfly and bird wings and for tropical fish.

I use novelty nature prints when I want a strong line, such as for leaf veins, but not as Broderie Perse, in which a very graphic shape is cut out and used as it reads on the fabric, such as an orange cut from a print featuring oranges. However, I will use unusual fabrics, such as a cabbage print that has light and shadows for small leaves, or highly textured prints for a bunch of lychee. I look for "zingers"—brash oranges and yellows with high contrast for the centers of flowers. It is worth spending time considering fabrics you might usually walk right by. Anything goes if it gives you the look you want.

Passionfruit and northern cardinal; detail of *Big Island Birds*, by Sylvia Pippen (page 42), and fabrics

Butterflies; detail of *Butterflies and Sashiko*, by Sylvia Pippen (page 43), and hand-dyed marbled fabrics by Marjorie Lee Bevis (see Resources, page 78)

Lychee; detail of *Big Island Birds*, by Sylvia Pippen (page 42), and fabric

Study both the fronts and backs of fabrics. Often, the reverse side of a fabric will have just the right lighter values you need.

Iris cut from right side of fabric; detail of *Wildflowers & Sashiko*, by Sylvia Pippen (page 46)

Iris cut from wrong side of fabric

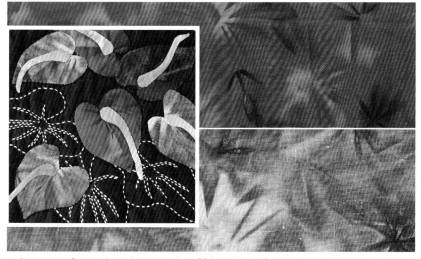
Anthurium cut from right and wrong sides of fabric; detail of *Tropical Sashiko Sampler*, by Sylvia Pippen (page 37), and fabric

When working with small appliqué shapes, the scale of patterns in print and hand-dyed fabric is important. Look for lines and a scale that suggest veins or the curve of a petal. Avoid solid fabrics, because they will make your appliqué shape look flat. Also avoid strong patterns, which can be distracting.

Open the fabric and step back to see how it looks from a distance. A fabric that may look variegated up close may read flat from a distance.

FINDING THE RIGHT PLACE TO CUT

It can be a bit overwhelming finding that sweet spot with just the right shading, light, and line in the midst of a large piece of cloth. Lay out the fabric and study it. You can use a chalk wheel to circle areas that might work. To isolate shapes in your fabric, use your Mylar template sheet, with the appliqué shapes cut out, as a window.

Mylar sheet window

fussy-cutting tip

With a permanent marking pen, mark your Mylar templates with any lines, curves, or areas you want to be light or dark. Use the markings to match up the lines or shading in your cloth.

Experiment! Your appliqué stash should look like Swiss cheese, with tiny, petal-shaped holes cut out of the heart of the cloth. I have a whole shoebox full of castaway petals that I dip into for other projects. It usually takes several tries to get it just right.

Cut out your appliqué shapes and audition them on the dark background with the Sashiko design transferred to it. The white transfer lines help you see what your Sashiko will look like and where the appliqué shapes fit. A design wall lets you step back to see how a fabric reads from a distance.

sashiko tip

Sashiko can be done either before or after appliqué shapes have been sewn down. However, if an appliqué shape is to be outlined in Sashiko, be sure to do the appliqué first.

Heliconia; detail of *Heliconia 'Sexy Pink,'* by Sylvia Pippen (page 43)

To make your appliqué look dimensional, place lighter petals in the foreground and darker ones in the background. Where two petals overlap, make sure there is contrast. Decide where the light is coming from and where shadow may be cast. As an example, look at *Heliconia 'Sexy Pink.'* The light is coming from below, so the stem of the heliconia flowers is darker above and brightly illuminated at the bottom.

With the lotus in *Tropical Sashiko Sampler*, however, the light is coming from the center of the flower, so the petals are darker at the tips.

Lotus; detail of *Tropical Sashiko Sampler*, by Sylvia Pippen (page 37), and fabric

innovative quilts *with* sashiko *and* appliqué

designing an innovative quilt with sashiko and appliqué

I encourage you to take the leap and design your own quilt combining Sashiko and appliqué. It's a challenge, but the rewards are so satisfying. You don't have to be a trained artist to come up with a strong design, especially in this age of digital cameras and photocopy machines.

Because I live in Hawaii, the Pacific cultural crossroads, my quilts are strongly influenced by Japanese and Polynesian art. However, Sashiko can be adapted to any pattern that catches your eye: a Southwest Indian blanket weave, Chinese fret designs, even tattoos! Great subjects for appliqué and Sashiko are everywhere in nature, we just need to open our eyes and take a closer look to see how we can capture its essence in cloth.

Polynesian quilts throughout the islands have common design elements: natural motifs, symmetry, contrast, and repetition with variation. Hawaiian quilts are cut snowflake-style from one piece of fabric folded in eighths. In Tahiti and other South Pacific islands, quilters fold their quilts in fourths and embellish them with embroidery and lyrical curved borders. I find it easier to design symmetrical quilts with stylized design motifs, because the patterns repeat and are predictable.

Orchid Tivaevae, by Sylvia Pippen. (Also shown on page 43.)

In contrast, Japanese art uses asymmetry to echo the unpredictable qualities of nature by placing designs off center, overlapping, or disappearing over the edge of a composition. Negative space is just as important as the design and is called *ma*, or aesthetic pause—a place for your eye to rest. These blank spaces are often filled with contrasting geometric patterns, flowing water, clouds, or mist designs, perfect for Sashiko or quilting. Japanese art will also often divide a design diagonally to draw the eye into and out of the composition without bisecting it evenly. Designing with asymmetry requires lots of experimenting, but it is a very gratifying process when your composition finally looks just right.

Try scattering patterns in a random way—the trick is to make them look irregular, yet balanced against the negative space created in between. Circles are considered harmonious and peaceful and are one of my favorite shapes to work with because they can stand alone, be formed first and scattered on a background, or be sewn into a pieced geometric quilt.

how to compose with your digital camera

My favorite design tools are my digital camera, a photocopy machine, and a big roll of tracing paper. Photos are a great way to study plants, second only to sketching while out in nature. I also use lots of reference material and haunt local libraries for ideas. It is tempting to use an artist's work you admire for inspiration, but don't rely on it solely, because it may influence your design too much and can involve complicated copyright issues. Use your own photos to get started designing, as they are original compositions and all yours.

1. With a digital camera in hand, meander through a garden, looking for plant forms and combinations that catch your eye. Use your viewfinder and zoom in to help isolate your composition. For appliqué flowers, pick an aspect that will translate easily into a simple appliqué shape. For Sashiko foliage, it is possible to capture more complicated aspects and intricate shapes (see Effective Sashiko Shapes, page 29).

2. One way to create your own composition is to cut flowers and foliage, arrange them on a dark fabric background, and photograph them (see page 28). I find it easier to envision the design if I can play around with placement using the real plant. You also get a chance to study the true color of the subject and to audition backgrounds.

Snap lots of photos; there's no waste in this digital age.

Auditioning flowers from my garden

3. Crop the photo in a photo-editing program and print it out in black and white. This saves ink. It also makes it easier to see the outlines of plants without being distracted by color.

4. Trace the outline shapes and some details of your photo. If it is hard to see the photo through the tracing paper, use a light table, tape it to the window, or put a light under a glass table. The tracing will show you whether the composition works or if you need to eliminate

flowers or leaves to simplify the picture. An outline without all the detail of color and shading should make sense to your eye.

Most photocopy machines reduce or enlarge and will copy a reversed image of a design drawn onto tracing paper. I like to use the same aspect of a flower and reverse it, simplifying the number of template shapes needed. Leaf or flower images can also be cut from the composition, reduced or enlarged, and moved around until it looks right.

5. Print in color the best photos you want to use for appliqué. These color photos will help you choose appliqué fabrics.

SIMPLIFYING SHAPES FOR APPLIQUÉ

Flower shapes are often very frilly or complicated. The trick is to capture the essence of the flower shape and aspect, yet make it simple enough to hand appliqué. Remember that you will add shading and dimension by cutting shapes from areas of your fabrics that suggest contour. If you are machine appliquéing, however, you can use much more complicated shapes, because you don't have to turn under the edges.

1. Place another piece of tracing paper over the original tracing of your flower as described at left. Trace the flower petals again and smooth out tight curves or serrated edges.

2. Study your drawing to see if it still reflects the aspect of the flower you want to express. If the center of the flower is very complicated, simplify it or leave it to be executed in embroidery embellishment later.

3. Pin your tracing to a wall. Darken the lines, if necessary, so you can really see the design well. Stand back to see if it works from a distance.

Freshly picked hibiscus

Simplified drawing

Hibiscus circle; detail of *Tropical Beauty*, by Kitty Pippen (page 38)

EFFECTIVE SASHIKO SHAPES

Unlike with appliqué, it is possible to outline more complicated shapes with Sashiko. After tracing leaves, trace the veining inside the leaf shape. The central and auxiliary veins are often what give the leaf dimension. Eliminate leaves with awkward features and reduce the number of overlapping leaves. Too many parallel Sashiko lines close together are very busy and confusing to the eye.

Taro leaves from garden photos

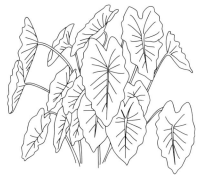

Simplified drawing

Taro leaves; detail of *Tropical Foliage Sashiko Sampler (page 41)*, by Sylvia Pippen

I rarely get the results I want from the first tracing. I tweak, enlarge, reduce, retrace, and try again.

auditioning the design

When you are satisfied with your design, transfer it to the background fabric (page 12), prepare the appliqué pieces using your preferred method, and pin the appliqué shapes in place on a design wall.

The white transfer lines give you a very good idea of how the Sashiko will look when it is finished, as will the appliqué shapes, especially if they are preformed with the press-over Mylar method (page 14). If some aspect of the design doesn't work, now is the time to fix it! Wash the transfer lines out of the background fabric or turn it over and use the back side if the fabric is reversible.

To help you get started, refer to Sashiko and Quilt Designs (page 72) for overall designs of water, bamboo, geometrics, Kamon circles, and borders. I encourage you to experiment with images from nature and to mix them with traditional designs.

embroidery embellishment

'Ohi'a Lehua and 'I'iwi Honeycreepers,
by Sylvia Pippen

planning the embroidery

Simple embroidery can bring a flower or bird to life. Details not possible to execute in fabric can easily be done with embroidery. I don't paint or draw details with permanent pens. Instead, I prefer to "paint" with embroidery stitches.

'Ohi'a; detail of *'Ohi'a Lehua and 'I'iwi Honeycreepers*, by Sylvia Pippen (page 30)

I use DMC embroidery thread, but feel free to experiment with finer threads, such as machine embroidery, crochet cotton, shiny rayon, or silk. Study a photograph of the object to determine color and form. These two elements are more important than perfect embroidery stitches, especially when embellishing flowers to look realistic. Look closely to see how the stamens curve or cross each other; try to capture their form with your embroidery stitches. The embroidery can make or break whether the flower looks dimensional or flat.

Choose color with enough contrast. Audition a strand or two of embroidery thread with your appliqué.

Does it show well from a distance? If not, adjust the contrast slightly. For very small details, I almost exclusively work with one or two strands of embroidery thread.

Columbine; detail of *Wildflowers & Sashiko*, by Sylvia Pippen (page 43)

Border; detail of *Orchid Tivaevae*, by Sylvia Pippen (page 43).

Use a stem stitch with a single strand of embroidery thread to create stamens in the center of a flower. I use two strands for French knots at the end of the stamens; try to choose a brilliant contrasting color to make them stand out. Fill in larger areas with satin stitch.

It is easier to embellish more stylized quilts because the embroidery stitches do not have to create perspective. It is important to keep your stitches even and consistent, especially when outlining appliqué elements. Some Tahitian-style quilts, including the border, are highly embellished with embroidery using a variegated six-strand DMC embroidery thread. I like to use #5 DMC perle cotton thread in-the-ditch between the border and body of a quilt.

embroidery stitches

You can add wonderful detail and dimension to any quilt using the three most basic embroidery stitches. The satin stitch, French knot, and stem stitch are used for the projects in this book.

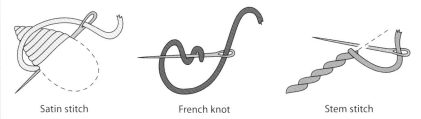

Satin stitch   French knot   Stem stitch

finishing techniques

layering and basting

1. Cut the quilt backing a few inches larger than the quilt top, piecing it if necessary. A quilt hangs best if the backing seam is centered vertically or if two seams are placed at equal distances from the side edges.

2. Iron the quilt back and quilt top. Spread the quilt back wrong side up on a flat surface. Center the batting over the quilt backing and place the quilt top on it, right side up. Try to keep the edges parallel to the edges of the backing.

3. Pin the layers together and thread baste in 2 directions, making a grid 4″–5″ apart. Baste with stitches no longer than ½″. Begin with a knotted thread and end by backstitching to secure it. Your basting needs to last as long as it takes to quilt your top.

4. Once your grid is finished, baste the edges of the sandwich together ¼″ from the edge. Trim the batting to within ½″ of the edge, so it will not snag or stretch while you work.

quilting

I am a lap quilter; I don't use a hoop or a frame. Because the quilt is carefully basted, I can start quilting anywhere on the quilt. I use the palm of my non-needle hand beneath the area I want to quilt to lift and smooth the quilt, then I anchor all the layers with a straight pin. I can then quilt up to the pin, move it to another spot, and continue. This keeps the quilt back flat and wrinkle free.

I usually quilt in the ditch right along seams around any pieced blocks, then around the appliqué, and next to sashing strips and borders. I quilt next to Sashiko designs enough to anchor the layers well. However, it is not necessary to completely outline Sashiko with quilting.

Many of my quilts are small, so I don't add a background quilting design behind the appliqué and Sashiko. On larger quilts, I do add geometric quilting patterns, such as diamonds or waves. I like to add Hawaiian-style echo quilting on my borders.

binding and facing

I use one of two methods to finish the edges of my quilts: binding or facing. A binding shows on both the front and back of the quilt, whereas a facing is turned entirely to the back. A faced quilt hangs very straight and gives a clean edge without introducing another design element.

Press the quilt, front and back, and trim the batting and backing even with the quilt top. Check your dimensions and square up as necessary. If trimming loosens the basting around the edge of the quilt, redo it so it doesn't shift when you bind or face your quilt.

BINDING

1. To bind a quilt, use 2″-wide double-fold strips cut on the straight of the grain. To join the strips for enough length to go completely around the quilt, sew a diagonal seam to prevent excess thickness in this area when the binding is turned.

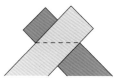

Sew diagonal seam.

2. Trim excess fabric and press the seam open. Fold the binding strip in half lengthwise, wrong sides together, and press.

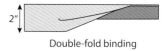

Double-fold binding

3. With raw edges even, position the binding on top of the quilt near the middle of one side. Leave the first 6″ of the binding unstitched and begin sewing with a ¼″ seam allowance. Stop stitching ¼″ from the first corner and backstitch.

4. Remove the quilt from the machine. Rotate the quilt so the stitching is at the top. To miter the corner, fold up the binding strip at a 45° angle to the corner. Fold the binding down along the next side, with raw edges aligned; use a pin to hold the fold in place.

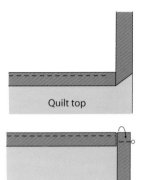

Fold binding up, then down.

5. Start stitching at the fold of the binding strip with a ¼″ seam allowance. Continue stitching along the edge of the quilt top. Stop within ¼″ of the next corner and backstitch. Repeat Step 4 to form a mitered corner. Stop stitching 6″ from the point where you began.

6. To connect the ends, fold the unstitched binding edges back on themselves, so they meet in the middle over the unsewn area of the quilt top. Press the fold.

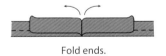

Fold ends.

7. Unfold both sides of the binding. Place the right end on top of the left at right angles. With right sides together, match the centers of the pressed X's. Draw a diagonal line

from the left corner to the right corner. Pin and stitch on the line.

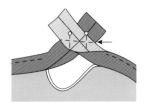

Match centers, draw diagonal line, pin, and stitch.

8. Trim the seam allowance to ¼″ and press the seam open. Refold the binding, press the fold, and stitch the rest of the binding to the quilt.

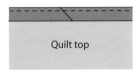

Stitch binding in place.

9. Fold the binding over the edge of the quilt, so it covers the stitching on the back of the quilt. As you fold the corner, a folded miter will appear on the front.

10. On the back, fold one side first, then the other, to create a miter on the back.

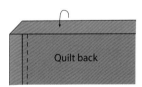

11. Hand stitch the binding to the back of the quilt with an appliqué stitch (page 19). Add a hanging sleeve.

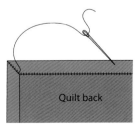

Fold binding to back and stitch.

hanging sleeve:

To add a hanging sleeve to a quilt with binding, follow these steps.

1. Cut a strip of fabric 8½″ wide and as long as the finished width of the quilt minus 1″.

2. Fold under each end of the strip ¼″ and stitch.

3. Fold the sleeve in half lengthwise, right sides together, and stitch along the long edge. Turn right side out and press.

4. Hand stitch the sleeve to the top of the quilt back, with the sleeve seam at the top where the binding meets the quilt back. Move the bottom edge of the hanging sleeve up ¼″ before hand stitching it to the quilt back, allowing space to insert a rod.

FACING

1. Cut 2″- to 3″-wide strips to equal the length of the sides of the quilt. The length and number of strips will depend on the size of the quilt.

2. With right sides together and raw edges matching, pin each side strip to the quilt top and stitch with a ¼″ seam allowance.

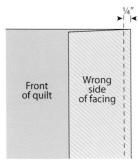

Stitch.

3. From the front side of the quilt, press the strip away from the seamline. Use a pressing cloth for dark colors. Topstitch the facing ⅛″ from the seam through all layers.

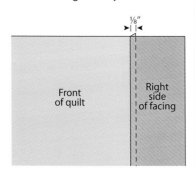

Press and topstitch.

4. Turn the quilt over. Fold the facing onto the back of the quilt, making sure a tiny edge of the quilt top rolls to the back. Press, using steam. Turn under the raw edge ¼″, and hand stitch it to the back of the quilt.

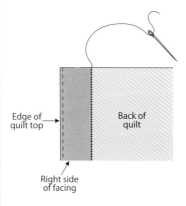

Fold facing to back and stitch.

5. Cut 2″- to 3″-wide strips 1″ longer than the finished width of the bottom edge of the quilt to create a finished corner. Be sure to measure the quilt after the side facings are attached. Turn the quilt to the front side.

6. With right sides together, stitch the bottom facing to the bottom edge of quilt, making sure the strip extends ½″ beyond the quilt at each end.

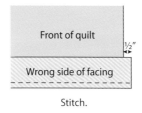

Stitch.

7. From the front side of the quilt, press the strip away from the seamline. Use a pressing cloth for dark colors. As before, topstitch ⅛″ from the seam through all layers. Fold the facing to the back of the quilt and press as you did for the sides. Fold in the excess facing at each end and stitch in place.

8. For the top edge facing, which will serve as a hanging sleeve, cut the strip(s) 5″ wide × 2″ longer than the finished quilt width. Be sure to measure the quilt after the side facings are attached. Sew this facing to the front top edge of the quilt, right sides together, allowing the facing to extend 1″ at each end.

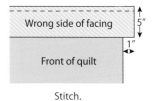

Stitch.

9. From the front side of the quilt, press the strip away from the seamline. Use a pressing cloth for dark colors. Topstitch ⅛″ from the seam through all layers.

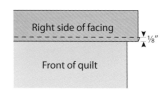

Press and topstitch.

10. Fold the 1″ extensions to the back of the facing strip and tack in place. Fold the facing to the back of the quilt and press well. Fold the long edge under ¼″ and hem. Leave the ends open so you can insert a rod or dowel for hanging the quilt.

Fold in ends.

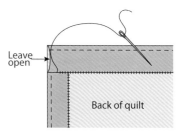

Fold facing to back, press, turn under long raw edge, and hand stitch.

quilt
gallery

Tropical Sashiko Sampler, 70″ × 70″, by Sylvia Pippen.

This quilt combines nine tropical flowers and sixteen traditional Japanese geometric designs. Left to right: heliconia, bird of paradise, hibiscus (top row); plumeria, lotus, ginger (middle row); anthurium, angel trumpet, moth orchid (bottom row). I drew the blocks from plants and photographs while working as a gardener at the National Tropical Botanical Garden on Kauai. (See Resources, page 78, for quilt pattern and fabric kit information.)

'Ohi'a Blossom,
8″ × 10″,
by Nancy Taniguchi.

Tropical Miniatures,
34″ × 34″,
by Kitty Pippen. A small
version of *Tropical Sashiko
Sampler* (page 37).

Tropical Beauty,
52″ × 52″,
by Kitty Pippen.

A variation of *Tropical
Sashiko Sampler* (page
37) using nine flowers
set in octagons and
Kamon crests.

Sylvia's Tropical Garden, 20″ × 44″, by Pat Reynolds.

Pat combined several patterns—heliconia, bird of paradise, moth orchid, ginger, and lotus—and embellished the centers of some flowers with beads.

Passionflower, 27″ × 37″, by Sylvia Pippen.

This quilt was inspired by passionflowers growing over a trellis in the National Tropical Botanical Garden on Kauai where I worked as a gardener. The flowers are embellished with embroidery and put in an oval frame to look like a botanical print. (See Resources, page 78, for quilt pattern information.)

Plumeria Floating on Water, 21″ × 32″, by Sylvia Pippen.

The water design is partially filled in with appliqué and can be done either by hand or by machine. The plumeria petals are doubled to give them more dimension. (See Resources, page 78, for quilt pattern and fabric kit information.)

Big Island Birds II, 39″ × 58″, by Sylvia Pippen.

This quilt uses Sashiko instead of appliqué to outline foliage behind the birds.

Tropical Foliage Sashiko Sampler, 60˝ × 60˝, by Sylvia Pippen.

This quilt uses light green Sashiko thread to outline nine Hawaiian plants. Left to right: traveler's palm, taro, lauhala (top row); monstera, bamboo, breadfruit (middle row); ti, 'laua'e fern, hapu'u tree fern (bottom row). All of these designs were drawn from photographs taken in my garden or in local botanical gardens on the Big Island. (See Resources, page 78, for quilt pattern and fabric kit information.)

Big Island Birds, 55″ × 75″, by Sylvia Pippen.

This quilt was a collaboration with my cousin, Susan Stanley, and my mother, Kitty Pippen. Susan designed the bird blocks, I executed them in cloth, and my mother and I worked the Sashiko designs and put the quilt together. (See Resources, page 78, for quilt pattern and fabric kit information.)

Butterflies and Sashiko, 22˝ × 24˝, by Sylvia Pippen.

This small wall quilt was inspired by a centuries-old Sashiko kimono of bamboo leaves, clouds, and stars. The butterflies are formed from Marjorie Lee Bevis marbled cotton (see Resources, page 78, for quilt pattern and fabric kit information).

Heliconia 'Sexy Pink,' 21˝ × 38˝, by Sylvia Pippen.

This quilt was inspired by a stand of heliconia and bamboo in Hanalei, Kauai. The sunlight filtered through the bamboo and lit up the lower dangling petals (see Resources, page 78, for quilt pattern and fabric kit information).

Orchid Tivaevae, 50˝ × 50˝, by Sylvia Pippen.

I made this quilt while living on our 40-foot sailboat, *Twilight*. The quilt was inspired by a quilt designed by Ruta Tixier Rarotong and was featured in *The Art of Tivaevae: Traditional Cook Islands Quilting*, by Lynnsay Rongokea. The stylized leaf patterns and cattleya orchids were appliquéd and then embellished with chain stitch, French knots, and stem stitch embroidery. The scalloped border is appliquéd. In contrast to Hawaiian quilts, Tivaevae are usually backed but not quilted. This quilt was quilted with a traditional Japanese Sashiko wave design to represent the blue Pacific Ocean.

Passionflower Lei, 45″ × 45″, by Sylvia Pippen.

The pattern is turned 90° clockwise and repeated in each corner, so the vines connect. The centers of the flowers are embellished with embroidery and the curved border edged with a stem stitch.

Broken Bamboo with Dogwood, 36″ × 41″, by Kitty Pippen.

Broken geometric Sashiko designs work well with any flowers.

Tropical Sea Life Sampler, 52˝ × 68˝, by Sylvia Pippen.

This quilt adapts traditional Kamon wave designs by adding sea animals and appliqué within the design. Marjorie Lee Bevis marbled fabric forms the schools of fish (see Resources, page 78). Hand quilted with clamshells and wave designs by Kitty Pippen.

Wildflowers and Sashiko, 42˝ × 58˝, by Sylvia and Kitty Pippen.

This quilt was a collaboration with my mother, Kitty Pippen. I designed the six wildflower blocks, and we worked together on the layout. Kitty put it all together and quilted it. Flowers, left to right: bleeding hearts, iris cristata (top); wild rose, rocky mountain columbine (middle); lupines and poppies and trillium (bottom).

tropical waves

FINISHED QUILT: 24½″ × 41″

Designed and made by Sylvia Pippen

The underwater world of Hawaii is as colorful as the coastline above, where Spinner dolphins can be spotted jumping and surfing the waves.

This asymmetrical quilt uses scattered wave motifs and diagonal schools of fish to pull your eye through the picture. Five traditional Japanese Kamon wave variations are worked in Sashiko on indigo and then appliquéd in circles to a graduated background that goes from the dark depths of the ocean to the turquoise blue above. The random waves on the background are quilted with a variegated thread to make them more visible. It took lots of playing around with placement and looking at negative space between the wave circles, then positioning and repositioning the fish and dolphins before it looked right.

I encourage you to experiment with your own composition. One of the many joys of appliqué is that you can fool around with placement and then step back to get a very good idea of how it will look when it's all sewn down. Audition your circles and appliqué fish shapes on your background fabric. Use the placement diagram (page 50) as reference if you want to duplicate this design.

materials

Yardage based on 42″-wide fabric.

See Fabrics for Appliqué (page 20). Avoid batiks with a high thread count for the Sashiko circles, because it is difficult to pull heavy Sashiko thread through batik.

- ⅓ yard or scraps of marbled gray fabric for dolphins
- ⅓ yard or scraps of marbled yellow fabric for angelfish
- ⅓ yard or scraps of mottled yellow-green and blue-green batik fabric for parrot fish
- ⅓ yard or scraps of multicolored marbled fabric for fins
- 1⅓ yards mottled blue-indigo fabric for borders and Sashiko wave circles
- ⅝ yard indigo to blue-green fabric for background
- 1⅓ yards for backing and facings
- 29″ × 45″ piece of low-loft batting
- White design transfer paper
- Japanese Sashiko needle or any sharp needle with a big eye
- 1 skein white Sashiko thread or #5 perle cotton
- Black DMC embroidery thread for eyes
- Cotton variegated blue-green machine quilting thread for machine or hand quilting

The dolphins are cut from a marbled fabric, using spots and splashes for eyes and linear lines to indicate the shape of the dolphins.

Dolphin fabric

The angelfish are cut from a single piece of marbled cotton, taking advantage of the swirls in the fabric to accentuate the lines of the fish.

Angelfish fabric

Note that the parrot fish school begins as light green-yellow and swims off the quilt in dark green-blue hues. The fins and tails are marbled cotton.

Parrot fish fabric

cutting

All measurements include ¼″ seam allowances.

Graduated indigo to blue-green fabric:

19″ × 36″ for background

Mottled blue-indigo fabric:

2 strips 4½″ × 33½″ for side borders

2 strips 4½″ × 25″ for top and bottom borders

5 squares 9″ × 9″ for Sashiko wave circles

Backing and facings fabric:

29″ × 45″ for backing

2 strips 2½″ × 41½″ for side facings

1 strip 2½″ × 26″ for bottom facing

1 strip 5″ × 27″ for top facing/sleeve

note

The project instructions are written for hand appliqué. For fusible machine appliqué, reverse the appliqué patterns, trace them onto the paper side of fusible adhesive, and fuse. Do not add the turn-under allowances.

sashiko wave circles

PREPARING

Refer to page 4 of the pullout for five wave patterns.

1. Center each Sashiko wave pattern on the right side of the blue-indigo squares and transfer the design (see Marking the Design, page 12).

2. Stitch the designs in white Sashiko thread (see Stitching a Sashiko Design, page 13).

STABILIZING WITH FREEZER PAPER

1. Using a compass or circle maker, trace and cut out a 7″-diameter circle from clear template plastic. Carefully center the circle over the right side of the Sashiko wave and mark the edges of the circle with chalk. Place pins

uniformly around the chalked circle to outline the circle on the back of the fabric.

2. Using the plastic template, trace and cut out a 7″ circle of freezer paper.

3. Center the freezer paper circle, shiny side down, on the wrong side of the Sashiko wave, using the pins around the chalk line to help align it. Iron in place. Remove the pins.

4. Cut the fabric around the circle, leaving a ¼″ turn-under allowance.

5. Baste the turn-under allowance over the edge of the freezer paper.

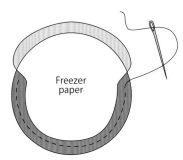

Baste seam allowance.

APPLIQUÉING

1. Using the placement diagram (page 50) as a guide, pin the wave circles in place on the background fabric. Appliqué the circles to the background.

2. Cut away the background fabric from behind the appliquéd wave circles, leaving ¼″ seam allowance.

Cut away background.

3. Remove the basting and then the freezer paper.

dolphins and fish

PREPARING

Choose your favorite technique from the Appliqué Methods (page 14).

Using the patterns on page 4 of the pullout, prepare and cut out 5 angelfish A, 6 big dolphins B–D, 3 little dolphins E–F, and 9 parrot fish G–J. Leave a ³⁄₁₆″–¼″ turn-under allowance for hand appliqué.

APPLIQUÉING

1. Referring to the placement diagram (right), appliqué the dolphins, angelfish, and parrot fish in place on the background fabric. Appliqué any shapes that overlap the borders after you sew on the borders.

2. Press from the wrong side and trim the top to 17″ × 33½″.

adding borders

1. With right sides together, stitch the 4½″ × 33½″ border strips to the sides of the quilt top. Press the seams toward the borders. Sew the 4½″ × 25″ border strips to the top and bottom edges of the quilt top. Press the seams toward the borders.

2. Appliqué the dolphins and fish that overlap the borders.

3. Referring to the pullout pattern (page 4) for placement, embellish the dolphin and fish eyes with 1 strand of black embroidery thread. I used a stem stitch (page 31) in a circle or spiral.

finishing

Refer to Finishing Techniques (page 32).

1. Layer and baste the quilt.

2. With thread that matches the background, quilt around the wave circles and just inside the quilt borders.

3. Trace the 8 wave curves K–R (pullout page 4) onto template plastic.

4. Lay out a section of the curve templates (pullout page 4) on the quilt top, using the placement diagram as reference. With a sharp, white chalk pencil, trace the top curves first, remove the templates, and continue to trace the remaining templates placing them so they completely cover the quilt top.

Lay out wave templates on quilt top.

5. Quilt the wave pattern by hand or machine with variegated cotton machine quilting thread.

FACINGS

Refer to Binding and Facing (page 33).

1. Use the 2½″ × 41½″ strips to face the sides of the quilt.

2. Use the 2½″ × 25½″ strip to face the bottom edge of quilt.

3. Use the 5″ × 26½″ strip to face the top edge and to complete the sleeve.

Refer to Tropical Sea Life Sampler (page 45) for another variation.

Placement diagram for *Tropical Waves*

Sea-grass and Fish, 29″ × 36″, by Sylvia Pippen (see Resources, page 78, for quilt pattern and fabric kit information).

Dolphins and Waves, 23″ × 40″, by Sylvia Pippen (see Resources, page 78, for quilt pattern and fabric kit information).

bamboo garden

FINISHED QUILT: 22½″ × 30½″

Designed and made by Sylvia Pippen

The ubiquitous hibiscus, Hawaii's state flower, adorns gardens and roadsides everywhere in the Islands.

Choose your favorite color scheme; hibiscus grow in almost every color except blue. Look for fabrics with color gradations and streaks that will make the petals look curved and that draw your eye into the center of the flower. Use a high-contrast "zinger" fabric for the pistil.

Heliconia are dramatic, pendulous flowers ranging in color from hot pink and yellow to deep orange. Look for mottled fabrics to capture light and shadows on every petal. I cut the hibiscus leaves from a print of hosta leaves; experiment with other graduated green fabric with linear lines. Sashiko creates the outline of the bamboo and fern foliage in the background.

Hibiscus fabric

Leaf fabric

Hibiscus fabric
(used in *California Poppies*, page 56)

Heliconia fabric

materials

Yardage is based on 42˝-wide fabric.

See Fabrics for Appliqué (page 20). Avoid batiks with a high thread count for the background because it is difficult to pull heavy Sashiko thread through batik fabric.

- ⅓ yard or scraps of streaked red fabric for hibiscus petals

- ⅓ yard or scraps of streaked yellow-orange fabric for hibiscus petals

- Scraps of bright yellow-orange mottled fabric for hibiscus center pistils

- ⅓ yard or scraps of mottled orange-red and purple fabric for heliconia

- ⅓ yard or scraps of green fabric with linear lines for leaves

- 1⅓ yards graduated indigo to blue-green fabric for background, outer border, and binding

- ¼ yard graduated light to medium blue batik for inner border

- ⅞ yard fabric for backing

- ⅓ yard for hanging sleeve

- 27˝ × 35˝ piece of low-loft batting

- White and dark design transfer paper

- Japanese Sashiko needle or any sharp needle with a big eye

- 1 skein white Sashiko thread or #5 perle cotton

- Thread for machine or hand quilting

cutting

All measurements include ¼˝ seam allowances.

Graduated indigo to blue-green solid:

1 rectangle 18˝ × 26˝

2 strips 3˝ × 22½˝ for top and bottom outer borders

2 strips 3˝ × 25½˝ for side outer borders

3 strips 2˝ × 42˝ for binding

Graduated light blue to medium blue batik:

2 strips 1˝ × 17½˝ for top and bottom inner borders

2 strips 1˝ × 24½˝ for side inner borders

Backing fabric:

1 rectangle 27˝ × 35˝

Hanging sleeve:

1 strip 8½˝ × 21½˝

note

The project instructions are written for hand appliqué. For fusible machine appliqué, reverse the appliqué patterns, trace them onto the paper side of fusible adhesive, and fuse. Do not add the turn-under allowances.

preparing the background

Center the pattern on page 2 of the pullout page over the right side of the background fabric. See Marking the Design (page 12) to transfer the flower, leaf, and Sashiko fern and bamboo motifs. If white lines do not show up, use dark transfer paper on lighter sections of background. Do not transfer the border lines.

appliqués

PREPARING

Choose your favorite technique from the Appliqué Methods (page 14).

Using the patterns on pages 1 and 2 of the pullout, prepare and cut out the number of pieces A–G shown below. Leave a ³⁄₁₆˝–¼˝ turn-under allowance for hand appliqué.

Red and yellow fabrics:

A1–A6: 2 of each

B1–B6: 2 of each

C1–C6: 2 of each

Mottled orange-red and purple fabric:

D: 1 and 1 reversed

E: 5 and 5 reversed

Green leaf fabric:

F: 4 and 4 reversed

G: 2 and 6 reversed

APPLIQUÉING

1. Referring to the pattern on the pullout (page 2) for placement, appliqué leaves F–G and petals A1–A6, B1–B6, C1–C6, D, and E in place. Leave the points of petal Er and leaf Fr loose until the borders are sewn onto quilt.

2. Press the quilt top from the wrong side.

sashiko background

1. Referring to Sashiko (page 7), use white thread to work Sashiko along the bamboo and fern lines.

2. Press, then trim the quilt top to 16½″ × 24½″, keeping the design centered.

adding borders

1. With right sides together, stitch the 1″ × 24½″ inner border strips to the sides of the quilt top. Press the seams toward the borders. Stitch the 1″ × 17½″ light blue/blue inner border strips to the top and bottom edges of the quilt top. Press the seams toward the borders.

note

Before adding the outer borders, refer to the quilt photo and note that the border color graduation is reversed from the background fabric.

2. With right sides together, stitch the 3″ × 25½″ outer border strips to the quilt sides and then the 3″ × 22½″ strips to the top and bottom edges. Press the seams toward the borders.

Quilt diagram

finishing

Refer to Finishing Techniques (page 32) .

1. Layer and baste the quilt.

2. With thread that matches the background, quilt in the ditch around appliquéd flowers and leaves. To emphasize the bamboo and fern design, quilt along the outside of the Sashiko.

3. Bind the quilt edges, adding a hanging sleeve.

california poppies

FINISHED QUILT: 16″ × 20″

Designed and made by Sylvia Pippen

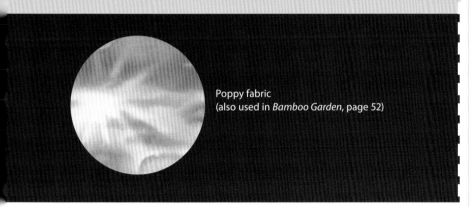

Poppies cover the green hills of the Golden State and are one of my favorite wildflowers.

This quilt is bordered in an oval frame and could be used as a centerpiece for a quilt, pillow, or handbag.

Poppy fabric
(also used in *Bamboo Garden*, page 52)

materials

Yardage based on 42″-wide fabric.

See Fabrics for Appliqué (page 20). Avoid batiks with a high thread count for the background, because it is difficult to pull heavy Sashiko thread through batik fabric.

- ½ yard dark solid for background

- ⅝ yard orange-purple batik for border

- ½ yard mottled brown-orange batik for bias inner border

- ⅓ yard or scraps of streaked white-yellow-orange for poppies

- Scraps of dark brown-orange for buds

- ¾ yard cotton for backing and facings

- 20″ × 24″ piece of low-loft batting

- White design transfer paper

- Japanese Sashiko needle or any sharp needle with a big eye

- 1 skein white Sashiko thread or #5 perle cotton

- 6-strand cotton embroidery thread—black, gold, yellow

- Chalk pencil

- Thread for machine or hand quilting

cutting

All measurements include ¼″ seam allowances.

Dark solid fabric:

14″ × 17″ for the background

Orange-purple batik:

1 rectangle 19″ × 23″ for the outer border

Brown-orange batik:

1 bias-cut strip 1″ × 40″ for the inner border

Backing and facings fabric:

20″ × 24″ rectangle for the backing

2 strips 2½″ × 20½″ for side facings

1 strip 2½″ × 17″ for bottom facing

1 strip 5″ × 18″ for top facing/sleeve

note

The project instructions are written for hand appliqué. For fusible machine appliqué, reverse the appliqué patterns, trace them onto the paper side of fusible adhesive, and fuse. Do not add the turn-under allowances.

transferring the design

Center the California Poppies pattern (page 4 of the pullout) on the dark background and transfer the design (see Marking the Design, page 12). Do not transfer the oval.

appliqués

PREPARING

Choose your favorite technique from the Appliqué Methods (page 14).

Using the patterns on page 4 of the pullout, prepare and cut out pieces 1–12. Add a ³⁄₁₆″–¼″ turn-under allowance for hand appliqué.

APPLIQUÉING

1. Appliqué poppy petals 1–4 and 5–8 and buds 9–10 and 11–12 in order onto the dark solid background.

2. Press from the wrong side.

embroidery embellishment

Using the pattern on the pullout as a guide, mark the centers of the poppies with a chalk pencil. With one strand of black floss, stem stitch the center of poppy 1–4. Stem stitch the stamens of both poppies in gold. Add a bright yellow French knot at the end of each stamen.

sashiko

See Sashiko (page 7) to work the poppy stems and leaves in Sashiko.

adding the oval border

PREPARING THE APPLIQUÉD BACKGROUND

1. Fold the appliquéd fabric in half lengthwise and then in half crosswise; lightly press the creases. The creases form registration marks for the center of the top, bottom, and sides.

2. Trace the pattern oval (pullout page 4) onto freezer paper and fold in half lengthwise and then in half crosswise. With a pencil, mark the center of the top, bottom, and sides.

3. Cut out the freezer paper oval (oval template).

4. Place the oval template shiny side down on top of the appliquéd piece, lining up the marks and creases to center the oval. Lightly iron and pin in place.

5. Use a chalk pencil to trace around the freezer paper oval. Remove the freezer paper.

6. With a ruler and a chalk pencil, measure and mark small dashes ¼″ *outside* of the traced oval. This will be the cutting line. Do not cut. Set aside.

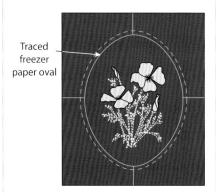

Traced freezer paper oval

Background

PREPARING THE BORDER FABRIC

1. Fold the border fabric in half lengthwise and then in half crosswise; lightly press the creases. Open and place the freezer paper oval template shiny side down on the right side of the border fabric, lining up the marks and creases to center the oval. Pin and iron in place.

2. With a chalk pencil, mark the creases at the center top, bottom, and sides outside the oval. Trace around the oval and remove the freezer paper.

3. Measure ¼″ all around the *inside* of the traced oval and mark with dashes. Carefully cut out this smaller inner oval from the border fabric.

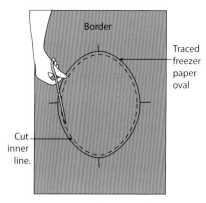

Border

Traced freezer paper oval

Cut inner line.

Cut out small inner oval.

ADDING THE INNER BORDER

1. Iron the 1″ bias strip in half lengthwise, wrong sides together, to form a ½″-wide double-fold bias strip.

2. Place the bias inner border strip on the appliquéd piece with the folded edge toward the appliqué, and line up the raw edges with the dashed outer oval. Pin the inner border in place, starting at the bottom center of the oval. Hand baste and machine stitch ¼″ from

the raw edge. Fold back the raw edges so the 2 ends meet at the bottom.

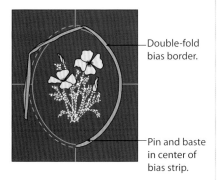

Double-fold bias border.

Pin and baste in center of bias strip.

Lay raw edges of bias strip on dashed outer oval.

3. With a chalk pencil, mark the top, bottom, and side registration marks on the inner border.

ADDING THE OUTER BORDER

1. Place the outer border face up onto the appliquéd background with the inner border attached. Line up all registration marks.

2. Pin in place around the oval, turning under ¼˝ of the outer border fabric to just cover the machine stitching line in the center of the inner border and exposing ¼˝ of the inner border.

3. Appliqué the outer border in place.

Turn under ¼˝ on outer border fabric and line up with machine stitching line. Appliqué in place.

TRIMMING THE BACKGROUND FABRIC

1. Turn the quilt top to the wrong side. Trim the excess appliqué background ¼˝ outside the oval on the dashed lines.

2. Press the seams toward the outside.

finishing

Refer to Finishing Techniques (page 32).

1. Layer and baste the quilt.

2. With quilting thread that matches the background, quilt around all the appliqué flowers and buds and around the perimeter of the Sashiko, right next to the Sashiko stitches.

3. Square up and trim the quilt to 16½˝ × 20½˝.

Refer to Binding and Facing (page 33).

4. Use the 2½˝ × 20½˝ strips to face the sides of the quilt.

5. Use the 2½˝ × 17˝ strip to face the bottom edge of quilt.

6. Use the 5˝ × 18˝ strip to face the top edge and to complete the sleeve.

Poppies and lupine from *Wildflowers and Sashiko* (page 46).

key fret sashiko and orchids

FINISHED QUILT: 26½˝ × 21½˝

Designed and made by Sylvia Pippen

Traditional Japanese art often uses geometric Sashiko designs with flowing shapes, such as water, flowers, or clouds.

In this project, an allover key fret design of Sashiko sets off sprays of orchids. The key fret, or silk weave, pattern was introduced to Japan from China on Ming-period textiles. Although this looks very complicated, it is actually one of the easiest geometric Sashiko patterns to stitch, because it is continuous. Use the key fret pattern or choose another geometric from Sashiko and Quilt Designs (page 72).

I used a very graphic pansy fabric for the orchids, fussy cutting the orchid centers from the pansy faces. The leaves are cut from a batik with linear lines.

Pansy fabric fussy cut for orchid centers and petals

Leaf and stem fabric

materials

Yardage based on 42˝-wide fabric.

See Fabrics for Appliqué (page 20). Avoid batiks with a high thread count for the background, because it is difficult to pull heavy Sashiko thread through batik.

- ⅝ yard solid dark indigo fabric for background

- ⅓ yard or fat quarter rose-red fabric with linear lines for orchid petals

- ⅓ yard or fat quarter pansy face or other flowered fabric that can be fussy cut for the center of the orchids

- ⅓ yard striped green batik for leaves and stems

- ¼ yard mottled green fabric for inner border

- ⅝ yard green batik for outer border and binding

- ⅞ yard for backing

- ⅓ yard fabric for hanging sleeve

cutting

All measurements include ¼˝ seam allowances.

Dark indigo fabric:

1 rectangle 21˝ × 17˝ for background

Backing fabric:

30˝ × 26˝ rectangle

Mottled green:

2 strips 1˝ × 14½˝ for side inner borders

2 strips 1˝ × 20˝ for top and bottom inner borders

Green batik:

2 strips 3½˝ × 15½˝ for side outer borders

2 strips 3½˝ × 26˝ for top and bottom outer borders

3 strips 2˝ × 42˝ for binding

Striped green fabric:

2 bias strips ⅝˝ × 12˝ for stems

Hanging sleeve:

1 strip 8½˝ × 25˝

note

The project instructions are written for hand appliqué. For fusible machine appliqué, reverse the appliqué patterns, trace them onto the paper side of fusible adhesive, and fuse. Do not add the turn-under allowances.

- 30˝ × 26˝ piece of low-loft batting

- White transfer paper

- Japanese Sashiko needle or any sharp needle with a big eye

- 1 skein white Sashiko thread or #5 perle cotton

- Thread for machine or hand quilting

transferring the design

Center the pattern (on page 1 of the pullout) over the right side of the background fabric rectangle. See Marking the Design (page 12) to transfer the design. Use a straight edge to transfer the key fret design.

appliqué

PREPARING

Choose your favorite technique from the Appliqué Methods (page 14).

Prepare and cut out petals 1–4 and P–Q for buds from the pattern (pullout page 1). Leave a ³⁄₁₆″–¼″ turn-under allowance for hand appliqué.

APPLIQUÉING

1. Fold the ⅝″ bias strips in thirds lengthwise to form stems. Press. Appliqué to the background, leaving ¼″ overlap allowance to be covered by the orchids and leaves.

2. Appliqué leaves A–O, buds P–Q, and orchid petals 1, 2, 2r, 3, 3r, and 4, in that order.

sashiko

1. The key fret pattern is continuous, so start working the pattern from the edges inward. It will be necessary to tie off or skip, leaving a loop on the back as you work around the orchids and leaves.

2. Press from the wrong side, squaring the corners, and trim the appliqué top to 19″ × 14½″.

adding borders

1. With right sides together, stitch the 1″ × 14½″ inner border strips to the sides of the quilt top. Stitch the 1″ × 20″ inner border strips to the top and bottom of the quilt top. Press the seams toward the border strips.

2. With right sides together, stitch the 3½″ × 15½″ outer border strips to the sides of the quilt top. Press toward the border. Stitch the 3½″ × 26″ outer border strips to the top and bottom of the quilt top. Press the seams toward the border strip. Square up the quilt top by trimming to 26″ × 21½″.

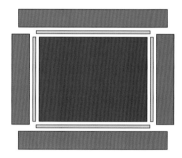

Assembly diagram

finishing

Refer to Finishing Techniques (page 32).

1. Layer and baste the quilt.

2. With thread that matches the background, quilt around the flowers, leaves, buds, and stems. Quilt in the ditch right next to the inner border.

Refer to Binding and Facing (page 33).

3. Use the 2″-wide strips to bind the quilt.

4. Add a hanging sleeve.

Cascading Orchid, 28″ × 37″, by Sylvia Pippen. A double Cypress fence geometric Sashiko pattern is used behind orchids.

rainbow plumeria

FINISHED QUILT: 30˝ × 30˝

Designed and made by Sylvia Pippen

Plumeria, or frangipani, are exquisite fragrant lei flowers that vary from alabaster white to butter yellow, from soft pink to deep red, or a blend called rainbow.

Duplicate the plumeria shown or choose your own color scheme. Plumeria can be made with single petals, or they can be doubled with a contrasting fabric to give them more dimension. This pattern uses single petals, cut with the curved pattern in the cloth so that each petal has a pink outer edge.

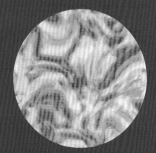

Plumeria fabric

The pattern is divided in fourths in Tahitian quilt style. Plumeria are placed over a stylized leaf design that has been appliquéd in each corner. In my quilt (page 63) the leaf motifs and curved border are needle-turn appliquéd; the plumeria are formed with the press-over Mylar method (page 14). The curved border is cut from a single piece of fabric, appliquéd, and stem stitched with embroidery thread.

materials

Yardage based on 42″-wide fabric.

- 1 yard mottled chartreuse for background
- ⅞ yard mottled dark green batik for plumeria leaves
- ½ yard yellow and pink fabric for plumeria
- ⅓ yard or scraps of white or other contrasting fabric for double-petal variation (optional)
- 1⅛ yards mottled green batik for curved border and binding
- 1 yard fabric for backing
- ⅓ yard fabric for hanging sleeve
- 34″ × 34″ piece of low-loft batting
- #5 DMC perle cotton dark green embroidery thread
- Thread for machine or hand quilting

cutting

All measurements include ¼″ seam allowances.

Background fabric:

33″ × 33″ square

Mottled dark green fabric:

4 rectangles 13″ × 18″

Mottled green batik:

31″ × 31″ for curved border

4 strips 2″ × 42″ for binding

Backing fabric:

34″ × 34″ square

Hanging sleeve fabric:

1 strip 8½″ × 29″

note

The project instructions are written for hand appliqué. For fusible machine appliqué, reverse the appliqué patterns, trace them onto the paper side of fusible adhesive, and fuse. Do not add the turn-under allowances.

preparing background fabric

1. Fold the square in half, right sides together, then in fourths, and in eighths. Press. The creased fold lines will be registration marks to align the 4 leaf appliqués.

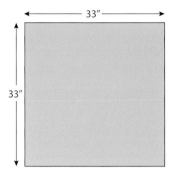

Background

Fold in half.

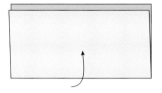

Fold in fourths.

Fold in eighths and press.

2. Unfold the square and lay flat.

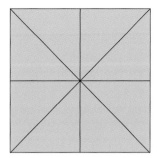

Background with fold lines

leaf appliqués

PREPARING

1. Trace the leaf pattern (page 3 on the pullout) onto freezer paper. Cut it out.

2. Fold the dark green fabric rectangles in half, right sides together, on the straight of the grain; press.

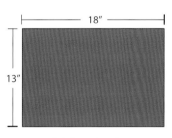

Fabric rectangle

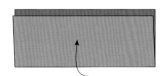

Fold in half.

3. Place the freezer paper leaf pattern on the fold, shiny side down. Iron and then pin in place.

Place template on fold.

4. Cut out the leaf shape, adding ⅛″ turn-under allowance.

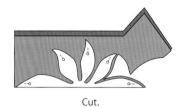

Cut.

5. Place the appliqué leaves on the background along the diagonal fold lines. Measure and align each outer leaf point the same distance from the corners. Place the larger leaf toward the center. Allow ⅛″ overlap for the turn-under allowance in the center where the leaf points meet.

APPLIQUÉING

1. Appliqué in place.

2. Press from the wrong side.

plumeria appliqués

APPLIQUÉING

Choose your favorite technique from the Appliqué Methods (page 14).

1. Using the patterns on page 3 of the pullout, prepare and cut out petals 1–5 and A–B for buds as instructed below. Leave a ³⁄₁₆″–¼″ turn-under allowance for hand appliqué.

Yellow and pink fabric:

1–5: 6 sets and 6 sets reversed

A: 20

B: 6 and 6 reversed

double petal plumeria

For high contrast, add an extra edge of white, bright yellow, or pink. Preform each petal with the press-over Mylar method (page 14) or paper template method (page 18) first.

1. Appliqué each petal to a square of white fabric, just along the edge for which you want to have a double petal.

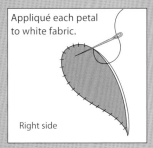

Appliqué each petal to white fabric.

Right side

2. Cut out the white fabric. Leave enough to turn under and to reveal the edge.

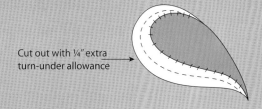

Cut out with ¼″ extra turn-under allowance

3. Place the petal template on the wrong side of the petal and offset enough to make the extra edge. Smooth the curve as necessary so the petal looks pleasing. Press.

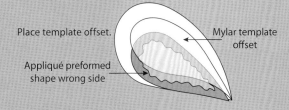

Place template offset.

Mylar template offset

Appliqué preformed shape wrong side

4. Appliqué in place.

Appliqué in place.

2. Refer to the quilt diagram (page 67) for appliqué placement. Appliqué buds A and B in place, allowing ¼″ or more overlap allowance where the bud tucks under the flowers. Excess can be trimmed just before appliquéing the petals over the buds.

3. If paper pieced or preformed with the press-over Mylar method, the 5 plumeria petals can be appliquéd together first and then put down as a unit.

tips

- To appliqué shapes together in your hand accurately, place preformed shapes on the pattern and glue baste them together where the petals overlap. Appliqué the petals together and trim bulky points.

- Temporary glue basting is a great way to hold down a long border or appliqué pieces. Use a bottle with a micro dropper so that only the smallest amount of glue is released. Do not place glue on or near your overlap allowance, because it can be hard to push your needle through the glue.

4. Appliqué plumeria petals 1–5 in order. Note that petal 5 tucks under petal 1.

5. On the wrong side, press the quilt top.

6. Trim to 31˝ × 31˝.

adding curved borders

1. Fold the border fabric square into eighths. Press.

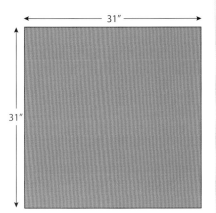

Border fabric

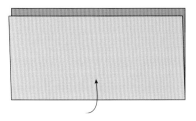

Fold in half.

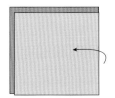

Fold in quarters.

Fold in eighths.

2. Trace the border pattern (pullout page 3) onto freezer paper and cut out.

3. Place the freezer paper border pattern on the folded fabric, aligning fold lines. Iron, pin in place, and cut out.

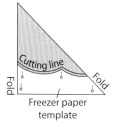

Position border pattern.

Quilt diagram

4. Unfold the curved border and place it over the quilt top, aligning the edges. Pin or glue baste in place.

5. Hand appliqué the curved border.

embroidery embellishment

See Embroidery Embellishment (page 30).

1. Using a stem stitch and dark green #5 perle cotton thread, work the background next to the curved border.

2. Turn over the quilt and press well from the wrong side.

finishing

Refer to Finishing Techniques (page 32).

1. Layer and baste the quilt.

2. Using quilting thread that matches the background, quilt around the perimeter of all the appliqué flowers, buds, and leaves. Echo quilt the background and border with stitch lines ½″ apart.

½″ echo quilting

3. Square up and trim the quilt to 30″ × 30″.

Refer to Binding and Facing (page 33).

4. Use the 2″ strips to bind the quilt. Add a hanging sleeve.

Waimea Plumeria, 42″ × 42″, by Sylvia Pippen. This quilt has double plumeria petals and buds.

Plumeria; detail of *Plumeria Floating on Water*, by Sylvia Pippen (page 40)

honeycreeper in bamboo

FINISHED QUILT: 20½˝ × 28½˝

*Designed and made
by Sylvia Pippen*

Apapane and 'I'iwi are native black and red honeycreepers that inhabit the rain forests around Volcanoes National Park on the Big Island of Hawaii.

The 'I'iwi have characteristic bright orange curved beaks and feed on bright red 'o'hia flowers as they flit through the rain forest canopy. With artistic license, I took one out of its native habitat and placed it among bamboo and monstera, both exotic but beautiful plants on the Big Island. The honeycreeper can be easily formed with the press-over Mylar method. The foliage is outlined in Sashiko with light green thread; white Sashiko thread could be used for more contrast.

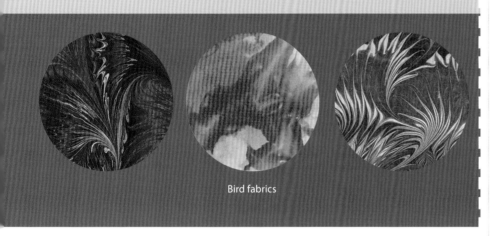

Bird fabrics

materials

Yardage based on 42″-wide fabric.

See Fabrics for Appliqué (page 20). Avoid batiks with a high thread count for the background, because it is difficult to pull heavy Sashiko thread through batik.

- ½ yard mottled dark green fabric for background

- ¼ yard light green/medium green graduated fabric for inner border

- ¾ yard green leaf batik for outer border and binding

- Scraps of marbled red fabric for bird

- Scraps of marbled black-and-white fabric for wings

- Scrap of orange-yellow for beak

- ¾ yard fabric for backing

- ⅓ yard fabric for hanging sleeve

- 25″ × 33″ piece of low-loft batting

- White transfer paper

- Japanese Sashiko needle or any sharp needle with a big eye

- 1 skein light green Sashiko or perle cotton #5 thread

- Medium-length Sashiko needle

- Yellow embroidery thread for leg

- Thread for machine or hand quilting

cutting

All measurements include ¼″ seam allowances.

Mottled green background fabric:

16″ × 24″ rectangle

Green graduated fabric:

2 strips 1″ × 21½″ for side inner borders

2 strips 1″ × 14½″ for top and bottom inner borders

Green leaf batik:

2 strips 3½″ × 22½″ for side outer borders

2 strips 3½″ × 20½″ for top and bottom outer borders

3 strips 2″ × 42″ for binding

Backing fabric:

25″ × 33″

Hanging sleeve fabric:

1 strip 8½″ × 19½″

note

The project instructions are written for hand appliqué. For fusible machine appliqué, reverse the appliqué patterns, trace them onto the paper side of fusible adhesive, and fuse. Do not add the turn-under allowances.

transferring the design

Center the pattern on the pullout page over the right side of the background fabric. See Marking the Design (page 12). Transfer the design omitting the outer border.

appliqué

PREPARING

Choose your favorite technique from the Appliqué Methods (page 14).

Prepare and cut out patterns 1–7 (on page 3 of the pullout). Leave a ³⁄₁₆″–¼″ turn-under allowance for hand appliqué.

APPLIQUÉING

1. Referring to the pattern on page 3 of the pullout, appliqué pieces 1–7 in order.

2. Use a stem stitch (page 31) to outline the bird leg and a satin stitch (page 31) to fill it in.

sashiko

1. Referring to Sashiko (page 7), work the bamboo and the leaves. Press from the wrong side.

2. Trim the quilt top to 13½″ × 21½″, keeping the design centered.

adding borders

1. With right sides together, sew the 1″ × 21½″ inner border strips to the sides of the quilt top. Press the seams toward the borders. Then sew the 1″ × 14½″ inner border strips to the top and bottom edges of the quilt top.

2. With right sides together, stitch the 3½″ × 22½″ outer border strips to the sides of the quilt top. Then sew the 3½″ × 20½″ strips to the top and bottom.

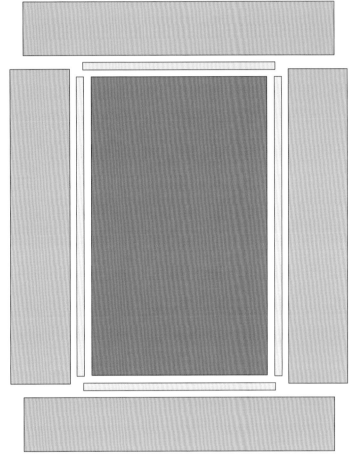

Quilt diagram

finishing

Refer to Finishing Techniques (page 32).

1. Layer and baste the quilt.

2. Using thread that matches the background fabric, quilt around the bird, outside the Sashiko leaves and bamboo, and just inside the inner border.

3. Use the 2″-wide strips to bind the quilt.

4. Add a hanging sleeve.

sashiko and quilt designs

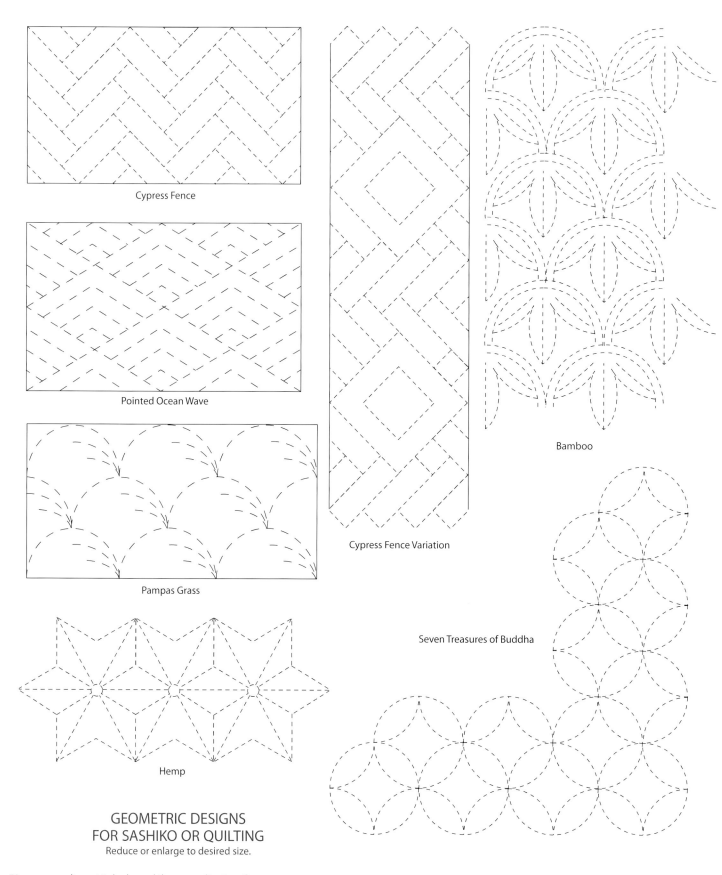

Cypress Fence

Pointed Ocean Wave

Pampas Grass

Hemp

Cypress Fence Variation

Bamboo

Seven Treasures of Buddha

**GEOMETRIC DESIGNS
FOR SASHIKO OR QUILTING**
Reduce or enlarge to desired size.

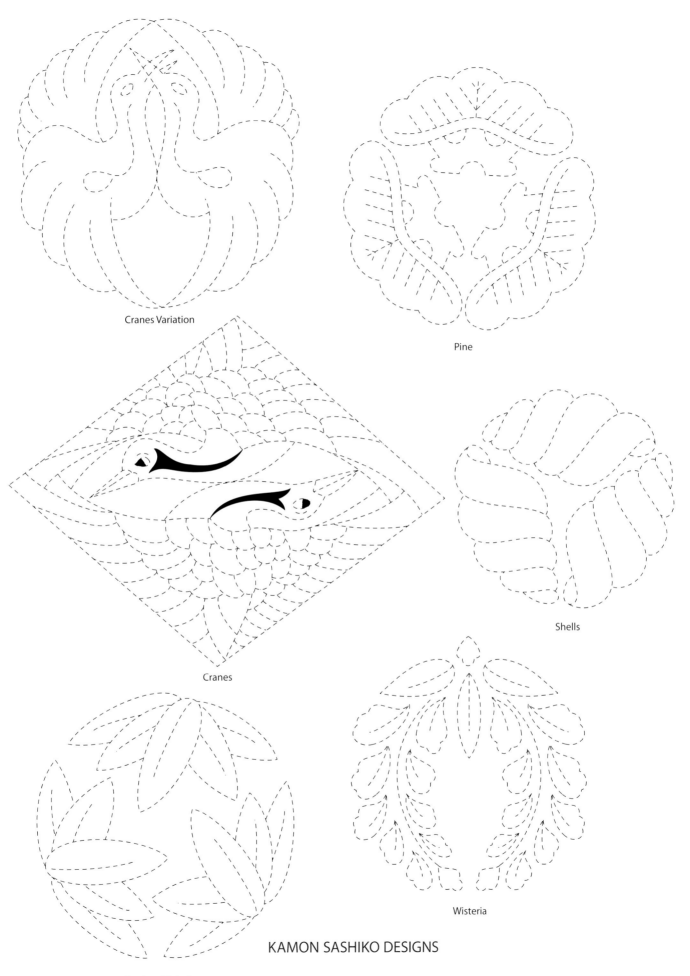

Cranes Variation

Pine

Cranes

Shells

Wisteria

KAMON SASHIKO DESIGNS

Bamboo Variation

BORDER DESIGNS FOR SASHIKO OR QUILTING

Oak

Maple

Ginkgo

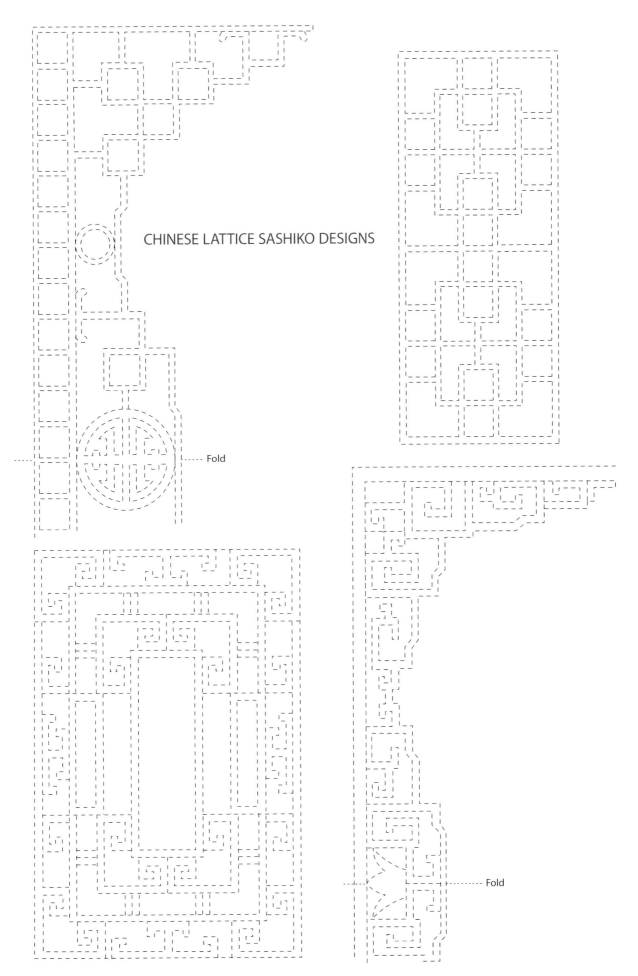

CHINESE LATTICE SASHIKO DESIGNS

Fold

Fold

BAMBOO LATTICE FOR SASHIKO AND QUILTING
Enlarge to desired size.

bibliography

Lynnsay Rongokea. *The Art of Tivaevae: Traditional Cook Islands Quilting.* Honolulu: University of Hawaii Press, 2001. Beautiful photography of Island women and their quilts.

Kitty Pippen, Sylvia Pippen. *Asian Elegance Quilting with Japanese Fabrics and More.* Seattle, WA: Martingale & Company, 2003.

Maggie Kate. *Ready-to-Use Oriental Designs: 495 Different Copyright-Free Designs Printed on One Side* (Dover Clip Art Series). Mineola, NY: Dover Publications, 1998.

Japanese Crests CD Rom & Book: 925 Royalty-Free Designs. Mineola, NY: Dover Publications, 2003

Matsuya Company. *Japanese Design Motifs.* Mineola, NY: Dover Publications. Invaluable source for Sashiko designs, with 4,260 illustrations of Japanese crests.

Japanese Designs (CD-ROM and Book). Mineola, NY: Dover Publications, 2002.

Kitty Pippen. *Quilting with Japanese Fabrics.* Seattle, WA: Martingale & Company, 2000.

Reiko Morshige and Kazuko Mende. *Sashiko: Blue and White Quilt Art of Japan.* New York: Kodansha America, Inc., 1991.

Joyce Hammond. *Tifaifai and the Quilts of Polynesia.* Honolulu: University of Hawaii Press. A scholarly description of the history of Polynesian quilts.

Susan Briscoe. *The Ultimate Sashiko Sourcebook.* Iola, WI: KP Books, 2005. An in-depth sourcebook that includes patterns, projects, and inspirations.

resources

Supplies

Mylar, patterns, and fabric kits
Sylvia Pippen
www.sylviapippendesigns.com

Sashiko thread, needles, and indigo and other Japanese fabrics
Maeda Importing
407-302-7172
www.maedaimporting.com

Loew-Cornell white transfer paper
www.dharmatradingcompany.com
or
www.CatalinaCottage.com

Marble cotton, silk, and accessories
Marjorie Lee Bevis
1401 Oakwood Drive
Oakland, OR 97462
541-459-1921
www.marbledfabrics.com

Appliqué thread
Superior Threads
#50 extra-long staple cotton thread
#60 polyester Bottom Line bobbins
www.superiorthreads.com

and

YLI
100% silk thread
www.ylicorp.com

Craft iron
Hobbico
Custom Sealing Iron
www.petersen-arne.com

Quilt stores in Hawaii

If you visit the Islands, check out our wonderful quilt shops for Hawaiian and Asian prints found only in the Islands, as well as batiks, patterns, books, and unique gifts. I teach at many of these stores, and they have ongoing classes that visitors are often welcome to join. It is a great way to meet local quilters.

Kauai

Kapaia Stitchery
3-3551 Kuhio Highway
Lihue, HI 96766
808-245-2281

Vicky's Fabrics
4-1326 Kuhio Highway
Kapaa, HI 96746
808-822-1746
www.vickysfabrics.com

Maui

Maui Quilt Shop
Azeka Shopping Center
1280 S. Kihei Road
Kihei, HI 96753
808-874-8050
www.mauiquiltshop.com

Sew Special
Queen Kaahumanu Center
Kahului, HI 96732
808-877-6128
www.sewspecialmaui.org

The Needlework Shop
505 Front Street, Unit 125
Lahaina, HI 96761
808-662-8554
www.theneedleworkshop.com

Hawaii Big Island

Topstitch
64-1067 Mamalahoa Highway #3
Kamuela, HI 96743
808-885-4482

Fabric Impressions
206 Kamehameha Avenue
Hilo, HI 96720
808-961-4468
www.fabricimpressions.com

Kilauea Kreations
Old Volcano Highway
Volcano, HI 96785
808-967-8090
www.kilaueakreations.com

Kilauea Kreations II
680 Manono Street
Hilo, HI 96720
808-961-1100
www.kilaueakreations.com

Quilt Passions
75-5626 Kuakini Highway, Suite 7
Kailua-Kona, HI 96740
808-329-7475
www.quiltpassions.net

The Fabric Workshop
1348 Kilauea Avenue
Hilo, HI 96720
808-933-1010

Oahu

Kaimuki Drygoods
1144 10th Avenue
Honolulu, HI 96816
808-734-2141
www.kaimukidrygoods.com

about the author

Sylvia Pippen grew up in the San Francisco Bay Area and was taught to sew at a very early age by her mother, Kitty Pippen. While raising her family in Shelburne Falls, Massachusetts, Sylvia studied tailoring and pattern making and designed jackets made with Japanese Yukatas and Seminole patchwork. Owner of a perennial flower nursery, Sylvia installed gardens, arranged flowers for weddings, and wrote weekly gardening columns for the local newspaper.

When her children were grown, Sylvia and Peter sold the 40-acre farm and bought an old 40-foot sailboat, where she learned to quilt in cramped quarters and to mend sails. Sylvia's quilts took on a tropical twist when she moved to Hawaii and worked as a gardener at the National Tropical Botanical Garden on Kauai. After co-authoring a book with her mother, Sylvia turned to teaching and designing patterns and fabric kits full time. She teaches locally, on the neighboring islands and on the mainland, while also managing her pattern and fabric kit business. Sylvia now resides in Hilo on the Big Island with her partner, Peter. When not quilting, she is weeding her garden, exploring the latest lava flow, snorkeling, or playing her flute.

Great Titles *from* C&T PUBLISHING

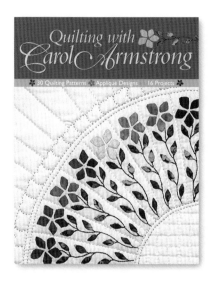

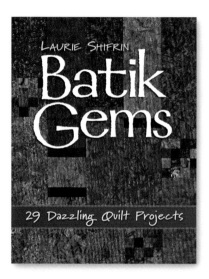

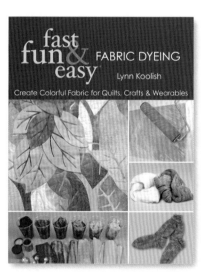

Available at your local retailer or **www.ctpub.com** *or* **800.284.1114**

For a list of other fine books from C&T Publishing,
ask for a free catalog:

C&T PUBLISHING, INC.
P.O. Box 1456
Lafayette, CA 94549
(800) 284-1114

Email: ctinfo@ctpub.com
Website: www.ctpub.com

C&T Publishing's professional photography services are now
available to the public. Visit us at www.ctmediaservices.com.

For quilting supplies:

COTTON PATCH
1025 Brown Ave.
Lafayette, CA 94549
Store: (925) 284-1177
Mail order: (925) 283-7883

Email: CottonPa@aol.com
Website: www.quiltusa.com

Note: Fabrics used in the quilts shown may not be
currently available, as fabric manufacturers keep most
fabrics in print for only a short time.